12

My
Anecdotal
Life

Also by Carl Reiner

Enter Laughing
All Kinds of Love
Continue Laughing
The 2,000 Year Old Man in the Year 2000 (with Mel Brooks)
How Paul Robeson Saved My Life and Other Mostly Happy Stories

Carl Reiner

My
Anecdotal
Life

a memoir

St. Martin's Press   ⚓   New York

www.stmartins.com

ISBN 0-312-31104-4

First Edition: May 2003

10 9 8 7 6 5 4 3 2 1

For Bessie Reiner
and her grandchildren—Rob, Annie, Lucas,
and her great-grandchildren—Jake, Nick, Livia, Romy, Rose

Contents

Acknowledgments

Thank you, Diane Reverand, Bess Scher, George Shapiro, Dan Strone, David Chasman, Mike Zimring, Sybil Adelman, Judy Nagy, Melissa Contreras, and always, Estelle Reiner.

Preface

More than once I've heard someone say, "Hey, Reiner, you ought to write those things down!" The most recent someone was Aaron Ruben, who said it as we walked to a parking lot. We had just spent a pleasant two hours having lunch at the West Coast Friar's Club and reminiscing about our life and times with a group of our peers, and one or two of our betters. At one o'clock that morning, just as I lay me down to sleep, Aaron's suggestion flitted through my mind, but I couldn't remember what it was that he suggested I "write down." Had it been a godly hour I would have called him and asked, but instead of awakening him, I awoke myself, made my way to the computer, and jotted down what Aaron had suggested, plus several more reminiscences that he may think worthy of including in this book, which I decided to call *My Anecdotal Life*.

These anecdotes are, for the most part, in the order that they popped into my head. I think that subconsciously I tried to orchestrate a literary "variety show." I have been asked, and have been tempted, to write an autobiography, but up to now,

I have opted to use my life's experiences to fuel the fictional *Dick Van Dyke Show,* and two semiautobiographical novels, *Enter Laughing* and *Continue Laughing.*

Except for the exclusion of the many mundane, unproductive, and boring stretches in my life, which have little or no entertainment value to anyone, I am offering *My Anecdotal Life* as my complete and official, abridged autobiography.

It is not necessary to read the chapters in order, but I recommend that you do, if you're interested in how a disorganized mind, when left alone, will somehow end up with something as organized as a book.

Inviting people to laugh with you while you are laughing at yourself is a good thing to do. You may be the fool but you're the fool in charge.

Carl Reiner—*My Anecdotal Life*

My
Anecdotal
Life

1

Sidney Bechet and His Jazz Band Meet Franz Kafka

It was the summer of 1942, I was twenty years old, World War II was raging, and in four months I would be a member of the U.S. armed forces. I spent that last, hot summer at Allaben Acres, an adult summer camp somewhere in the Berkshires. For ten dollars a week, as a member of a resident troupe of performers, I was required to and eagerly did the following:

Tuesday Night Games

I emceed such popular audience-participation games as pass the orange and a half dozen others that I have blotted from memory. I do remember being told that I was "very good at it."

Wednesday Night Campfire

I did a dramatic reading from Richard Wright's play, *Native Son*. My rendition of the defense attorney's impassioned summation to the jury never failed to garner me a sitting ovation.

Thursday Night Classic Musicales

Accompanied by a full chorus, I sang the baritone solo in George Kleinsinger's and Earl Robinson's "Ballad for Americans" (Paul Robeson's version was far superior). Later that season, I soloed again in Walt Whitman's "I Hear America Singing." The pianist-conductor, Vivian Rifkin, complimented my voice and my ability to sing on-key and in rhythm for many of my solos.

Friday Nights

I acted as host for the extraordinary jazz concerts.

Saturday Nights

I performed in the weekly musical revue, doing comedy sketches and acting as straight man to comedian Bernie Hern. One year later, Bernie acted as best man at my one and only wedding.

The Friday night concerts and the Saturday musical revues were extraordinary for many reasons, the foremost being that they featured the legendary Sidney Bechet and his band. It was unusual for a jazz artist of Sidney Bechet's renown to be performing at a resort as unrenowned as Allaben Acres. Sidney Bechet had just returned from Europe, where he had been widely admired and lauded. A street had been named after him in Paris, and in Antibes a bronze statue was erected in his honor. So why would such an esteemed artist accept so lowly a gig? Well, it was 1943, and Sidney Bechet and his great sidemen were "Negroes," and Negroes were still waiting for their slice of the American pie. The integration of the armed forces and all professional sports, including baseball, football, basketball, tennis, and golf, was still a dream. The management at Allaben Acres, being a progressive lot, offered the jazz icon Sidney Bechet the opportunity to "break the color line" by signing on as band leader and bringing his sidemen to live amongst and perform with white folk, for much less money than they deserved, I'm sure.

All of the cast members, especially jazz aficionados Bernie

Hern, scenic designer Paul Petroff, and his assistant, Estelle Lebost, were thrilled to have Sidney Bechet in their midst. Even though I knew little about jazz, their enthusiasm was so contagious that I was thrilled to be among people who seemed to know what to be thrilled about. It was their appreciation of the Arts that led to my involvement in introducing Franz Kafka to Sidney Bechet and his jazz band. Here now is how it came to pass:

It was a dark, humid, Thursday—the cast was onstage in the casino rehearsing for our Saturday night revue. We had just finished staging the song "Oh, You Can't Make Love in a Bunk for Eight," a comedy number written by Lewis Allan (a.k.a. Abel Meeropol, the composer of "Strange Fruit"), when the black, roiling clouds that had been threatening to explode all morning exploded. Lightning and thunder heralded the torrent of water that fell from the sky and crashed onto our casino roof, the dining room, and the dozens of roofs that housed the two hundred guests.

Herewith is an exchange that led to this fond remembrance.

"What's for lunch today?" someone asked.

"Meat loaf!" someone else shouted above a thunderclap.

"I love meat loaf," I think I said, "but not enough to risk getting my ass singed by a lightning bolt."

"Summer storms usually don't last too long," the amateur weatherman among us suggested. "It'll let up."

"Yeah," an optimist concurred, "it's one of them cloud-bursts that unbursts itself fast."

We soon learned that it was not "one of them cloudbursts" but a cloudburst of biblical proportions.

"Any of you cats know how to build an ark?" one of the musicians quipped.

After fifteen minutes of steady downpour, it was apparent

that the heavy rain was not only not letting up but coming down harder and harder.

"Hey, I got an idea," I distinctly remember Paul Petroff saying, "I got this great book, *The Metamorphosis* by Franz Kafka."

"It's sensational," Bernie concurred.

"Did you read it?" Paul asked.

"I gave it to you!"

"Oh, that's right, you said it was a classic! I just started it," Paul continued excitedly, "and it's a gas! Bernie, while we're waiting for the storm to pass, why don't you read it to us?"

"Good idea, but Carl's the actor, let him read it," Bernie suggested, "he's got better diction."

"Right! Carl, you're on!" Paul announced, "C'mon, we'll go to my room!"

Spurred by Paul's enthusiasm and lacking anything better to do, like lemmings, Bernie, Estelle, Sidney Bechet, trumpet player Bill Goodwin, trombonist Sandy Williams, two other members of the esteemed Bechet band, and I followed Paul and shoehorned ourselves into his bedroom. Think stateroom scene in the Marx Brothers' movie *A Night at the Opera* and you'll have a picture of how cramped the quarters were.

Paul Petroff, a most creative artist, lived backstage in a reclaimed storage room. To relieve the claustrophobia he must have felt sleeping in a dollhouse-sized bedroom, Paul had painted a blue-skied mural on the walls and, with phosphorescent paint, had created a star-studded ceiling. A single bed, an end table, a ratty club chair, and a jerry-built drawing board took up four-fifths of the floor space. Paul deferentially offered Sidney Bechet the stuffed club chair and bade his other guests to "plop down anywhere!" which they did—on the bed, on the floor, and on the wooden folding chairs our host dragged into the room. Paul then placed a stool at the foot of the bed and said, "Sit!"

"Here," he said, handing me a slim book, "you're on!"

"Remember, Kafka is a genius," Bernie warned, "so read with expression."

Paul and Bernie were respectively seven and eight years older than I. I so admired their sophistication, knowledge, and intellect that I would do anything to please them. Hungry for their approval, I was not sure that my sight-reading Kafka's classic was the way to get it, mindful that my reading the book badly could reflect negatively on Bernie and Paul's literary judgment and my reputation as an actor. I scanned the first few sentences and then looked at the faces of my querulous audience. They seemed to have as little faith in me as I should have had in myself. So, unarmed, unprepared, and for some reason, undaunted, I summoned up my best stage diction and began to read.

" 'The Metamorphosis, by Franz Kafka. One morning, upon awakening from agitated dreams, Gregor Samsa found himself, in his bed, and transferred into a monstrous vermin.' "

"Into a what?" Sandy Williams interrupted, wincing.

"A monstrous vermin," Bechet explained, "that's a big rat!"

"I know what vermin is, but how did this Samsa guy turn into a monstrous rat?"

"Or a big cockroach—roaches are also vermin," Bernie Hern volunteered.

"Is that what the guy turned into?"

"If you let the man read," suggested the quiet-mannered trumpet player Bill Goodwin, "maybe we'll find out."

That opening sentence hooked everyone, including me. From the first few pages we learned that Gregor Samsa was a fabric salesman who one morning found that he was unable to turn over and get out of bed. He would be late for work, because his back had become "a hard shell of armor" and his two legs had been replaced by "many wretchedly thin legs" that "danced helplessly before his eyes." Subsequently, we learned of his painful attempts to roll off the bed and onto the floor, and of his unsuccessful tries at manipulating his many skinny legs in climbing up the side of a wooden wardrobe. At this point we all agreed that Gregor had metamorphosed into a cockroach who was trying to convince his parents and boss through his locked bedroom door that he was fine, even though he was late for work and his voice sounded strange, like "an animal voice."

As the bizarre tale of a man turning into a giant cockroach unfolded, the rapt attention of my captive audience was often disturbed by someone needing clarification.

"Hold on, hold on," I recall Sandy Williams, calling out, "read that part again—where he climbed up the wall to that picture of a lady—and squeezed himself against the glass. . . ."

I read it again, and he shook his head.

"What's he got on those weird little legs," he asked, "some kind of stickum, or little suction cups?"

"Let the man read!" Bechet said gently.

Sandy allowed me to read a bit but jumped when I got to the part where Mr. Samsa tried to get his son out of the room by throwing little red apples at him.

"Whoa, did you just say," he asked in disgust, "that one of them apples *lodged* in roachman's back?"

I nodded.

"How the hell," he asked, disbelievingly, "could an apple get *stuck* in his back? What kind of back does that cockroach have?"

"Maybe he got quills like a porcupine," Sidney Bechet suggested.

"Sidney, did you hear Carl read anything about quills?" Sandy argued. "I didn't."

I suggested that if I read on we might get some useful information about his back. In Chapter Three, we did—we learned that the imbedded apple was, "a serious injury from which he suffered for over a month" and "since no one had the nerve to remove the apple, it stayed lodged in his flesh."

"Lodged in his *flesh*!" Sandy shouted, "Not *on* his *quills*!"

"Rotting there for a month!" Bechet added, "pretty damned disgusting!"

A lively discussion ensued, and all contributed.

"Howd'ya like to have a rotten apple festering in your back?"

"I wouldn't want a rotten apple festering anywhere in my body."

"How about a festering peach on your butt?"

"Hey, you're all making me nauseous!"

Not wanting to spoil anybody's appetite for lunch, I suggested that I stop reading.

"Over my dead body," Sandy Williams threatened, "I gotta know what happens to the cockroach-man."

"Carl, you just keep reading!" Bechet ordered.

"There are more than forty pages to go," I said, "and the rain seems to be letting up."

"Let it let up!" Sandy argued, "You ain't goin' nowhere till you finish this muthuh!"

"We may miss lunch," I warned.

"If you don't start readin'," Bechet warned, "we'll miss dinner, too."

I had never had a more attentive or appreciative audience in my young career. I read the last half of the book with a feeling of pride and empowerment. Until that afternoon, I had no idea that I could sight-read a whole novel without making any major gaffes. From the applause and the continuing discussion, I felt that I had done very well—but maybe not. That was sixty years ago and until recently, when the president of New Millenium Audio asked me if I would like to record *A Connecticut Yankee in King Arthur's Court,* no one had asked me to read another book. Unlike Paul Petroff, who only asked me to read that one book, New Millenium Audio has since contracted with me to do a half dozen of Mr. Twain's great works. To be honest, though, Paul Petroff has done more to make my life richer and fuller than any audio company ever could. Besides suggesting I read *The Metamorphosis* aloud, Paul had earlier, at one fateful Saturday night dance, told me about his new, late-arriving, shapely brunette assistant, Estelle Lebost. His exact words were, "Be nice to her, ask her to dance!" I did as I was told—I asked her to dance, and I was nice to her all that summer. That was fifty-nine years ago, and I am still being nice to her, as she is to me.

2

The Phar-Reaching Phart

I have had many heightened moments in my life, some pleasant, some painful. This is one of the painful ones. I am aware that the spelling of the word phart *is not the commonly accepted one. I chose it to avoid offending the more gentle of my gentle readers.*

I was born in apartment number 27 of a Bronx apartment building on the corner of Belmont Avenue and 179th Street. In 1922, my mother, like most immigrant women, chose to give birth at home where she could be sure that the child she breast-fed and smothered with love would be of her and her husband's blood and not some total stranger's. Horror stories of babies being switched at birth by careless nurses in over-crowded wards were too rampant to ignore. Home delivery, of course, posed some dangers, but my parents were comforted by the knowledge that three years earlier my mother had suc-cessfully delivered my brother, Charlie, by the same Dr. Neuschatz in that same apartment and in that same bed.

Charlie, in effect, was my stalking horse, and in the years to come, he continued to be that for me.

I spent my kindergarten and first-grade years attending the ancient, overcrowded Public School 57, which was located two blocks away between Belmont and Crotona Avenues. By the time I was ready to enter the third grade, the construction of a new school, just a scant three hundred yards from my home, was completed, and I became one of the first pupils to attend P.S. 92.

Before I entered kindergarten, I was considered a bright child simply because my father, whom my mother called Irving and I called Papa, took the time to teach me how to print my full name, recite the alphabet, and fill a page with numbers from one to a hundred. For appearing to be gifted, I was invited to skip half of first grade and go right to second grade. My parents proudly accepted the invitation. This decision and a later one that sent me to rapid-advance classes at Junior High School 45, by which I gained a full year, had a profound effect on me.

I graduated from Evander Childs High School in June of '38 at the age of sixteen. Being a year and a half younger and light-years less mature than my sexually adventurous peers made me feel like an outsider, a feeling that still dogs me. But hey, who's complaining! Being an "outsider" has given me the quiet time to ponder ways to behave like an "insider," which I think I have mastered.

My first day at P.S. 92 was a traumatic one. That morning, I awoke with a slight nausea and no appetite. My mother, or Bessie, as my father called her, was able to coerce me into eating a big bowl of hot cereal by reminding me that "all over Europe people are starving to death!" After wiping stray grains of Wheatena from my face with a damp dishtowel, my mother straightened my knitted blue tie and then walked me to school. Before abandoning me in the schoolyard, she ran a comb through my hair and warned me to "be careful!" and "pay attention to the teacher!"

With hundreds of other pupils, I waited anxiously for someone in charge to tell me where to go. That someone turned out to be a thin, stern-looking woman who, in a deep authoritative voice, introduced herself as Mrs. Mahler.

"Stop all that talking this minute!" she ordered, "Now form two lines in front of me—in size place, quickly, quickly!"

We formed the two lines and size-placed ourselves as best we could, which was not good enough for Mrs. Mahler. She grabbed a few misfits by the shoulder, dragged them to their proper place in line, and shoved them in. She announced that she was our third-grade teacher and ordered us to follow her to our spanking-new classroom. I was not happy with my new teacher, my new school, or the bloated feeling in my stomach. Mrs. Mahler instructed us to "find any seat for now and sit down!" I found the one farthest from her desk and sat in the last row. In Miss Thomas's second-grade classroom, I had sat in the first row. Miss Thomas was very different from Mrs. Mahler. Miss Thomas was really pretty and spoke with a soft voice. She liked me. My classmates called me teacher's pet, which I hated.

Miss Thomas had once asked for volunteers to be in a Christmas show she planned to put on in our classroom. A petite blond girl volunteered to tap dance, and a tall boy said he would like to sing a song. Miss Thomas, disappointed that there were only two volunteers, asked if there was anyone else who could do something to entertain.

"I can put both feet behind my head," I shouted out, "and walk around on my hands!"

Without being asked, I demonstrated my talent for Miss Thomas. The class giggled, then laughed, and applauded loudly. For an encore, I kept one leg behind my head and hopped around on the other one. Miss Thomas thought it so entertaining that she arranged to take our little show on tour. We played the kindergarten and first-grade classrooms. At the risk of appearing immodest, I must say that my contortionist act garnered the most applause and, more importantly, a big approving smile from Miss Thomas.

As I watched the sour-faced Mrs. Mahler take a fresh piece of chalk from a box, I could never envision myself becoming her pet. However, I did find a way to distinguish myself in her classroom. It was soon after we had settled in our seats that Mrs. Mahler told us how lucky we were to be going to such a beautiful new school and hoped we would find some way to show our appreciation for having been given this opportunity. At this moment, a huge, ear-shattering, triple-flutterblast of a phart escaped from me. The huge breakfast I had force-fed myself to help out the poor people in Europe who were starving to death had backfired. The laughter I had received for my contortionist act in Miss Thomas's class was nothing compared to the reaction I evoked by passing wind. The room full of third-graders were doubled over with laughter and couldn't hear, or refused to hear, Mrs. Mahler screaming at the top of her lungs, *"Beeee quiyyyet!"*

"That was not funny!" Mrs Mahler shouted, *"and will not happen again—not in my class!"*

She looked about the classroom and glared at everyone. It appeared that she glared at me with the same intensity and for the same length of time as she did the other pupils.

She doesn't know who pharted, I thought, *she doesn't know!*

When Mrs. Mahler sat down at her desk and cast a quick, knowing glance my way, I knew that she knew!

For the six months I was in Mrs. Mahler's class, I avoided making eye contact with her. I never raised my hand to ask a question or to answer one or to ask permission to use the boy's room. Whenever I chanced to see her in the halls, I either hid behind someone or turned and walked the other way. I never thought to share my feelings of shame and embarrassment with anyone. I kept my guilty secret for a long time, but ultimately, I, like all immature adults, was able to find the loud passing of gas to be funny. When I first saw the now-famous pharting fugue Mel Brooks so tastefully orchestrated for his film, *Blazing Saddles,* I laughed louder and longer than most people in my age group.

3

My First Best Job

Before I sat down to have breakfast this morning, September 14, 2002, I had not intended to write "My First Best Job." My plan was to begin the process of putting the chapters of this book in some kind of order. I was having the last spoonful of oatmeal when I read in the obituary section of *The New York Times* that William Warfield, a man I had known fifty-five years ago, had passed away at the age of eighty-three. It saddened me. It was 1947 when he and I trouped together in the road company of the Broadway musical revue *Call Me Mister.* Seeing his name triggered a raft of memories, memories too dear for me not to include in *My Anecdotal Life.*

William Warfield deserves a much fuller documentation of his life and musical triumphs than I am prepared to give him in this reminiscence. Anyone standing in the wings each night for a year as I did and hearing his rich bass-baritone voice sing "The Red Ball Express" and "The Face on the Dime," could have prophesied that Bill Warfield would someday become a great concert artist. He starred as Porgy in *Porgy and Bess* and inherited Paul Robeson's role in the film remake of

Show Boat. I would not have foreseen the international acclaim he would receive for his interpretations of German songs (*lieder*), but then I am not all that musical, as I admit in Chapter 8.

The cast for *Call Me Mister* was chosen at open auditions for actors, singers, and dancers who had served in the armed forces and were honorably discharged. Bill Warfield, Bob Fosse, Buddy Hackett, and Howard Morris were among the group of performers who were chosen by that process, but I found my way into the show through a back door.

I had been discharged from the army eight months earlier and had been unable to find a job. My wife, Estelle, and I lived on our unemployment checks. Her check, for having worked at Sperry-Rand as an isometric draftsman, drawing three-dimensional blueprints of planes and tanks, was $31 a week, and mine was $21 a week for my work securing our country's freedom by touring the Pacific in an army musical entitled *Shape Ahoy!*

Our combined $52 a week was just enough to buy food, some clothes, and pay the rent on our two-room sublet apartment in a Ninety-seventh Street brownstone. During my three-and-a-half-year army career, I had a fair amount of success as a comedian and hoped someday to work in nightclubs. I was anxious to go to these clubs and see the reigning comedians. The most written-up and talked-about comedian at that time was a fellow named Danny Thomas. He had been a tremendous hit at the 21 Club in Chicago and was now packing them in at Le Martinique, an elegant restaurant-nightclub on West Fifty-seventh Street. It was out of our league, as our entertainment budget allowed for moviegoing but no upscale nightclubbing.

While Danny Thomas was setting records at Le Martinique,

I was traveling downtown every day to try to see agents who might get me in to see producers who might be interested in allowing me to audition for a part in a play, a musical, a radio show, or a lowly club date. After one of my unproductive sorties, I stopped in to the Walgreen's Drugstore on the corner of Forty-fifth Street and Broadway to call my wife and tell her that I had struck out again. Walgreen's was known to all out-of-work actors as *the* place to go when you had no place to go. It was a place to find a kindred spirit willing to discuss "the sad state of the theater" and "how impossible it is to find a good agent, or a part in a good play, or a producer who recognizes talent when he sees it."

Walgreen's also sported the longest and busiest bank of phone booths in the city, phone booths that some actors treated as their private offices. After telling Estelle I was coming home unemployed and depressed, I hung up and started to leave. I stopped when I noticed a small black change purse lying on the floor of the booth. I picked it up, opened it, and found a veritable fortune, twelve dollars! The purse had most likely fallen out of some woman's pocketbook. I was torn between turning it in to one of the cashiers or turning it into two dinners and a show at Le Martinique. I decided on the cashier, because that's what my father would have done. It was the right thing to do. I snapped the purse shut and carried it and my newspaper in my right hand. My trench coat was draped over my left arm, and I carried my snap-brim fedora in my left hand. I wouldn't blame you if you're thinking, "Why is he boring us with these stupid details? Who cares what he's wearing or in which hand he's carrying his newspaper?" but these seemingly unimportant, inert items soon took on a life of their own.

My resolve to give the purse to the cashier was firm. As I

approached the cashier's station, I slowed to listen to an internal debate on good and evil that I was having.

DR. JEKYLL

Hey, look! There are three cashiers on duty.

MR. HYDE

Yes, and to which one will you give the purse?

DR. JEKYLL

The most honest-looking one, of course!

MR. HYDE

And which one is that?

DR. JEKYLL

I don't know. They all look a little . . .

MR. HYDE

. . . like they can't be trusted to return the purse to its rightful owner? You know, there is nothing in the little purse that identifies the owner.

DR. JEKYLL

What are you suggesting?

MR. HYDE

I'm suggesting that they'll keep it. The woman who lost it probably has no idea where she dropped it.

DR. JEKYLL

Are you saying that I don't turn it in? . . .

MR. HYDE

Turn it in, and you turn down the opportunity to see Danny Thomas at Le Martinique!

After wrestling with my conscience, the part of me that *had* to see Danny Thomas at Le Martinique told my conscience to shut up. I didn't fully accept the decision to keep the purse, so I kept it in my hand. The Dr. Jekyll in me was hoping that the woman who had lost the purse would be standing at the cashier's station, and I would say, "Oh, good, I was just about to give it to a cashier." While I was thinking this, Mr. Hyde was walking me to the door.

In trying to leave Walgreen's, I morphed into the Man of a Thousand Thumbs. I fumbled getting on my trench coat, pulling the purse and newspaper through one of the sleeves. I dropped my hat, retrieved it, and spent an inordinate amount of time moving my hat, my paper, and the purse from hand to hand as I struggled with the belt of my trench coat and my conscience. It seemed like hours before I finally made it through the revolving door. No thief, except for Woody Allen in *Take the Money and Run*, has ever made a more graceless and bumbling getaway.

My wife and I went to Le Martinique that night and sat at the very back of the club. For eleven dollars and a dollar tip, we had the cheapest item on the menu and saw a brilliant comedian-storyteller whose mesmerizing performance forced me to reconsider my plan for a career in nightclubs.

Very soon after our night of stolen pleasure, I secured an agent, Maurice Lapue, who handled promising young talent at MCA, one of the two big agencies in town. He arranged for me to audition for the job of social director at the Lake Spofford Hotel in New Hampshire. Maurice Lapue came by his shiny, black, slicked-down hair legitimately. In an earlier life, he and his wife had been a successful adagio dance team, Maurice and Cordoba.

The audition took place in one of the small conference rooms in the MCA office complex. I was prepared to do some of the comedy routines I had developed in the army, and some I had cobbled together since becoming a civilian. I had an audience of two, Mr. Abe Jacobson, an elderly, sour-faced hotel owner, and Mr. Lapue, the adagio-dancer-turned-agent. I remember doing my foreign radio commercials in French and Italian double-talk; a takeoff of an English drawing-room comedy, playing multiple parts; and a piece that I had performed in the army, "Monty the Talking Dog," a talented canine who did surefire impersonations of movie stars. For roughly thirty minutes, neither Mr. Jacobson nor Mr. Lapue moved a muscle. A rivulet of flop sweat ran down my chest and pooled in my navel as Abe and Maurice stared at me stone-faced. I had asked them if they'd heard enough and, amazedly, they shook their heads and, in unison, said, "Keep going! Keep going!"

Midway through my act, another unsmiling face peeked into a small window in the entrance door. I had no idea who this eavesdropper was, but since the room was soundproof, he was more like an eyedropper. As soon as I finished the nightmarish audition, Lapue and Jacobson started to confer, but Maurice stopped when a tapping on the little window got his attention. It was the eyedropper beckoning Maurice to come out into the hall.

Being alone with someone who had just sat through your whole comedy act without cracking a smile could be added to the dictionary as a definition for the word *uncomfortable*. Abe Jacobson squinted at me for a long moment before he spoke. He said something that had never before been said to me.

"Mr. Reiner," he offered, pontifically, "you seem to me . . . to be a very resilient young man!"

"Well, thank you, that's very uh . . ."

I had no idea what the heck he was talking about.

"Young man, you spend a summer with me at Lake Spofford," he said, breaking into a smile, "and with your resilience and my experience in coaching young comedians, I can predict a big future for you in our business."

I wasn't sure whether he meant the hotel business or show business. I told him that I was surprised he thought so well of me since I didn't hear him laugh even one time.

"I laugh internally when I'm concentrating," he explained. "Just so you know that I'm a man who puts his money where his mouth is, the salary is one hundred twenty-five dollars a week for ten weeks, and—are you married?"

"Yes, I am!"

". . . and room and board for you and the missus."

Wow! One hundred twenty-five dollars a week! Un-friggin-believable, to borrow an army expletive. The most money I had ever made in my life!

No sooner had Mr. Jacobson said that he would work out the details with Maurice Lapue than a serious-faced Maurice returned, hurriedly discussed the deal with Mr. Jacobson, complimented him on being "a very perceptive judge of talent," and sent him on his way.

"Carl, while you were auditioning," Maurice said, smiling devilishly, "did you notice a man looking through that little window at you?"

"Yes, I did. Who was that?"

"Herman Levin, the co-producer of *Call Me Mister*."

"Oh, great, I read that he's holding open auditions. I was going to the theater—"

"You don't have to go anywhere, he wants you to play the Jules Munshin part in the road company!"

"Oh, sure," I said, laughing, "the man looking in that little window wants me to play the lead in *Call Me Mister*. He couldn't hear a word I was saying!"

"No, Carl, he couldn't *hear* you, but he could *see* you, and he liked what he *saw!*"

Impossible as it may sound, that is exactly why I was hired. Herman Levin saw an actor who moved, gesticulated, and looked very much like Jules Munshin, the actor whose performance in the show had made him a star overnight. Within a short time, both Jules Munshin and his co-star, Betty Garrett, were in Hollywood playing alongside Frank Sinatra and Gene Kelly in the film version of the hit musical *On The Town*.

I couldn't believe it! Herman Levin had allowed me to bypass the open auditions and hired me, "sight unheard" and without consulting his co-producer, Melvyn Douglas. I thought, "Boy, this Herman Levin guy is some gambler!" I later learned that he was also some negotiator!

What a day! Two good offers for two good jobs from one lousy audition.

I told Maurice that I preferred to work on the legitimate stage rather than on a casino stage.

"You can do both," Maurice informed me. "Rehearsals for the show don't start until mid-September. You'll be finished at Lake Spofford by the end of August."

My postwar prospects, in one short afternoon, had gone from dismal to dizzying.

It was the happiest of happy times! I was happy doing at Lake Spofford the kind of social directing I had learned to do four years earlier at Allaben Acres. I was happy that my stand-up routines were well received and that Mr. Jacobson was happy that I was as resilient as he knew I'd be. Best of all, both Estelle and I were happy to know that she was pregnant. We received that news soon after I signed for the two jobs. How much happiness can one man take? Obviously all he can get!

If you guessed that this unfettered happiness is ultimately met by a counteracting dose of despair and disappointment, you are mostly wrong but a little right.

After an absolutely glorious summer of good work, good eats, a daily dose of the magnificent view of the White Mountains, and one vain attempt at playing golf, I was itching to start my first job as a paid-up member of Actors Equity!

Before starting rehearsal, Herman Levin requested that I meet with him to discuss my deal, but before I describe that meeting, I thought that it might be interesting to list all of the jobs and all the emoluments I had received before I signed to do *Call Me Mister*. If I were not computer semi-illiterate, I would have illustrated my work history with a nicely designed graph, but this will have to do.

Salaries earned from June of '38 to November of '47		Salary Per Week
1938: shipping clerk	Eleanor Frocks	$12.00
1938: shipping clerk	Rose-Lou Frocks	$10.00
1939: delivery boy	Weglinsky Machine Shop	$8.00
1939: actor	Gilmore Theater	$0.00
1939: actor	Gilmore Theater	$1.00
1940: actor	Rochester Summer Theater	$0.00
1941: actor	Rochester Summer Theater	$0.00
1941: actor	NYA Radio Workshop	$5.56
1942: actor	Avon Shakespearean Company	$30.00
1942: actor	Allaben Acres	$10.00
1942: chorus	*The Merry Widow*	$37.50

SALARIES EARNED FROM JUNE OF '38 TO NOVEMBER OF '47		SALARY PER WEEK
1942: soldier	United States Army	$54.00 per mo.
1943–1945: soldier	United States Army	$66.00 per mo.
1946: emcee	Lake Spofford Hotel	$125.00 per wk.

Which brings us to 1946, and the spirited negotiation my agent and I had with Herman Levin, anent a leading role in the road company of *Call Me Mister.*

HERMAN LEVIN

Carl, did you see the show?

ME

Before I left for the summer—you were kind enough to give me two free tickets. Sensational show!

HERMAN LEVIN

And a sensational part for you, right?

ME

Right!

HERMAN LEVIN

So, how much will you pay to play that sensational part?

[*Those were* Herman Levin's *exact words, and he stared at me waiting for an answer.*]

ME

Well, as much as I would love to play the part, I can't afford more than fifty dollars a week.

HERMAN LEVIN

Tell you what, instead of *you* paying *us*, how about signing a run-of-the-play contract and *we* pay *you* two hundred dollars a week to start, and, if you're not dismissed after two weeks, we'll up your salary to two hundred fifty.

[*I looked at* Maurice, *who nodded his approval, and I started to nod mine but stopped when* Herman Levin *held up his hand.*]

HERMAN LEVIN

Before you take the deal, there is one proviso. Under no circumstances are you to petition me for a raise. Two hundred fifty dollars a week is it! I don't want you sending me your great reviews from out-of-town critics and saying you deserve a raise. I expect you to get great reviews—if you don't get great reviews, you're not doing your job—and should give us a refund.

I accepted Herman Levin's deal and signed the contract. We opened in New Haven, played a week, then a week in Philadelphia, then the important opening in Boston. The financial success of the entire tour depended on how well we did here.

Opening night at the Shubert Theater was an exciting and exhilarating experience. From the opening number, in which we hear a trainful of returning servicemen sing "This Train Is a Goin' Home Train," to every sketch and musical number that followed, we could feel and hear the audience's approval. At the curtain calls, the applause that greeted each principal as he or she stepped forward was loud and prolonged. We all were hoping that this first-night reaction would translate itself into at least a month's run at the Shubert.

The following evening, after reading the rave reviews that the show and all its performers received in the local newspapers, including the "important for business" review in the *Boston Globe*, our beloved stage manager, Biff Liff, who went on to become a force on Broadway, shouted to everyone as we came through the stage door, "Send out your laundry!"—an old show business phrase that trumpeted a long run, a phrase that has become obsolete with the advent of one-day service.

The show ran not a month but almost five months, and broke a twenty-five-year-old record for touring companies held by *The Student Prince*. I could not imagine life getting any better than this. A lead in a hit show, a loving, pregnant wife, *and* a career-enhancing opportunity *right next door*!

Adjacent to the Shubert Theater was the Hotel Bradford and its famed nightclub, the Bradford Roof. Their marquees were side by side. One read *Call Me Mister* and the other, Now Playing at the Bradford Roof, Willie Shore. One afternoon, Maurice Lapue called from New York and proposed a deal he insisted that I not pass up—a week's engagement at the Bradford Roof!

"Think about it, Carl," he pitched, "your name on two marquees. *Call Me Mister* with Carl Reiner at the Shubert, and Now Playing at the Bradford Roof, Carl Reiner! In person in both places! Nobody has ever had his name on two side-by-side marquees!"

I was flattered, frightened and, at twenty-four, fearless but not feckless.

"Maurice," I pointed out, "you know that my name isn't on the Shubert marquee."

"It will be as soon as I call Herman Levin. He's no dope—he'll see its publicity value."

"Maybe, but I don't see how I can do eight shows a week . . ."

"Carl, the curtain comes down at eleven-oh-five, you leave your makeup on, change into a tux, run upstairs, and do a midnight show."

Maurice could not convince Herman Levin to put my name on the marquee, but he convinced me that playing the Bradford Roof was the opportunity of a lifetime. He arranged for me to see Willy Shore at his midnight show. What I saw was a man in total control of his material and his audience. He "killed the people," as the saying goes, and I realized that with my material, I couldn't even harm the people. I told Maurice that playing the club might be a problem.

"What's the problem? The money? Two bills, almost what you get from *Mister*—and for less work."

"No, the problem is that I don't have a real nightclub act."

"Just do what you did at Lake Spofford."

"It's not a polished act, and I don't have opening and closing songs, like all nightclub comedians have."

"So, polish up your act and find a couple of songs—you got a whole week before you open. Problem solved!"

I spent the week choosing material that I thought would be appropriate for the gig and found not an opening song but a calypso song that I thought amusing, "Men Smart, Women Smarter."

Scattered about the club on the exciting opening night were many of the cast members of *Call Me Mister,* among them Bob Fosse, Betty Kean, Howard Morris, and Buddy Hackett, who were there to support me, and they did. They all laughed louder and applauded longer than they would have were they being honest.

The following day, Buddy Hackett, who went on to become one of the truly great nightclub performers, shook my hand and told me that I "really stank." I learned from that engagement that I was not cut out to be a nightclub comedian. I hold in awe those chosen few who, night after night and year after year, stand up in clubs and make audiences scream with laughter. Of the old guard, at their best, there were none better than Buddy, Shecky Green, Danny Thomas, Milton Berle, Jack Carter, Jackie Miles, Jan Murray, Alan King and later, George Carlin, Richard Pryor and Bill Cosby, who took stand-up comedy to a new level. I'm sure I left out some great comedians who deserve to be mentioned, and I assume you're adding them to my list right now.

The sad thing about the Bradford Roof engagement is that, even though I was bad, the business was good enough for them not to fire me. I had to honor my contract and finish out the long, looooooooooong week.

Two weeks before ending our run in Boston and going on the road to play in Buffalo, Toronto, Detroit, and Cleveland for a week each, Estelle, who was now in her ninth month, left our Boston apartment and returned to her mother's Bronx apartment to await the arrival of our baby—who checked in at Beth Israel Hospital on Saturday night, March 6, 1947! I received that happy news backstage, right after the show's finale. I was able to fly down, late Saturday night, there being no show on Sunday, and see my wife and Robert, the healthy, six-pound, twelve-ounce baby boy whom we had wrought, and she had delivered. It was a happy time for us but not an easy time, especially not for Estelle, who had been in hard labor for thirty-eight hours while I was jumping around on a stage in Boston. That weekend, I stayed long enough to see that Estelle had weathered a difficult birth, and that it was worth the effort. Robbie was a beautiful, alert baby, and an excellent nurser.

A word in praise for my wife. In those days, among modern mothers, there were very few who considered nursing their babies. Most pediatricians made themselves indispensable by encouraging new mothers to make their lives easier by bottle-feeding their babies. A nursing mother has no need to pay the good doctor a weekly visit to adjust her baby's formula. Estelle actually had to scrounge around for information about how to breast-feed a baby, a primary function that is as natural as . . . breast-feeding! She got it not from her pediatrician but from her friend, Bessie Smith, a black social worker who was raised in the South, the home of breast-fed people. She recommended *The Rights of Infants,* a slim, great how-to book that still sits on a bookshelf in our home.

You may think that I am spending an inordinate amount of time on this subject, but if it weren't for breast-feeding, there was little chance that our new little family would have been together for a memorable, year-long road tour. When Estelle joined me in Chicago, Robbie was six weeks old. I had missed four weeks of his first days on earth, but in the next six months, I missed only the hours I spent performing at the Blackstone Theater.

Before arriving in Chicago, the show was wonderfully received in the four cities we played, and my reviews were such that I was tempted to send them to Herman Levin and ask him to reconsider the no-raise-under-any-circumstances oral contract he had coerced me into making with him. Two incidents occurred that gave me even stronger motivation to dishonor our producer's ironclad edict. Someone had sent Biff Liff, our stage manager par excellence, a column from the

Chicago Tribune that was written by Claudia Cassidy, the paper's esteemed, all-powerful drama critic. I ask your indulgence while I attempt to counteract the effects of my dismal failure at the Bradford Roof with a positive personal story that still thrills me to recall.

Claudia Cassidy had seen *Call Me Mister* on Broadway and hated everything about it. For some dark reason, we shall never know why, she wrote a particularly venomous critique of the wondrous Jules Munshin. He had to have done something unspeakably horrid to her to have provoked such vindictiveness. Miss Cassidy had suggested in her article that if the road company was anywhere near as bad as the one playing on Broadway, then we would do ourselves and the local theatergoers a service by bypassing Chicago or just closing down.

The management was nervous, as well they should have been. The show's financial success depended on a Chicago run at least as long as the run in Boston. To add to the cast's anxieties, on the eve of the Chicago opening, our leading lady, Betty Kean, comedienne and tap dancer extraordinaire, and much beloved by the company, had flown to New York for a short weekend visit that turned out to be a long forever visit. She would not be coming back to the show, and no one had a clue as to why she made this untimely decision. Subsequently, we learned that she was pregnant and had been advised by her doctor that her pregnancy would be jeopardized if she continued performing the strenuous musical and dance numbers.

We arrived in Chicago on Sunday, which gave us two whole days to find and rehearse a suitable replacement for our multitalented leading star. To find someone who could do the comedy sketches and sing and dance as well as Betty seemed an impossible task. The management solved it by hiring two people to do her part. Marilyn Day, a beautiful young singer with a thrilling voice, would do the musical numbers, and Charlene Harris, a versatile comedienne and one of the understudies, would perform the comedy sketches. In two days, by rehearsing as hard as Ruby Keeler did in *Forty-second Street*, Marilyn and Charlene made themselves ready for our Tuesday opening.

If we were lucky, Claudia Cassidy, who had suggested we bypass Chicago, would bypass our show. No such luck. On opening night there she was, sitting in her usual seat, pad in hand, ready to break our hearts and destroy the producer's dreams of another record-breaking run.

That night's performance turned out to be one of our very best. The emotionally charged cast members, all pulling hard for our two courageous, underrehearsed replacements to succeed, caused a company-sized adrenaline rush. We all knew we were "doing good," the audience knew we were "doing good"—but did the person with the poison pen recognize this, or would she tell our potential ticket buyers we "did rotten" and to spend their money elsewhere? During the performance, Biff Liff kept an eye on Miss Cassidy as she scribbled notes on her program. He was looking for some clue to her mood, but she sat solemn faced. Midway through the second act, she dropped a not-too-subtle clue by springing from her seat, bolting up the aisle and out the theater.

The following morning, Claudia Cassidy's review was one that none of us was anxious to read. She started by writing that "nine times out of ten the duplicate of a hit Broadway show is usually inferior to the original," and reiterated how she had disliked some of the performances in the original cast. She went on to say that what she saw at the Blackstone Theater last night "deserved a salute!" She singled me out and heaped upon me the kind of praise an actor dreams about getting from anyone, but especially from a hard-nosed critic. In praising me, Miss Cassidy took a sadist's pleasure in revisiting Jules Munshin's performance and ripping him again. Jules Munshin, who had a prodigious talent and was a bona fide sensation in New York, could easily have sued her for slander and won.

The last line of the unexpected review, which I am copying from a brittle Dead Sea Scroll-like, browned newspaper clipping dated May 15, 1947, reads: ". . . but most of all, Mr. Reiner, who easily could have his name in lights if that were the true reward of stardom."

If ever there was a time and a reason to reopen salary negotiations, it was that moment! Because Betty Kean's roles were being performed by two actors, I became the nominal comedy star of the show. I didn't get my name in lights, but I was now listed first in the program's Who's Who in the Cast. However much I was tempted to ask for a raise, I honored Herman Levin's edict, no raises, no matter what, and went about my business—and business was great! Everything about Chicago was great—and exciting, especially my new role as a father.

For the six-month Chicago run, Estelle and I lived with our baby in a one-room apartment at the New Lawrence Hotel. We slept on a Murphy bed that we pulled down from the wall the first day we moved in and kept down for the entire stay. We cooked on a two-burner hot plate that was set up in a small alcove, in which were crammed a small sink and a small refrigerator. One might call our quarters cramped, but *very, very* cramped would be more accurate. However, we were too happy and too involved in learning how to raise an infant to feel anything but lucky to be where we were.

After a few weeks, the show was on its tracks. Performing it every night and twice on matinee days was still pleasurable but had become routine. On the other hand, the backstage dramas were anything but routine. Two of the performers—Bob Fosse and his dancing partner, Marian Niles—fell in love and became life partners—temporary life partners, as it turned out. Robbie attended his first big church wedding when he was three months old. I have an eight-millimeter film record of the bride and groom coming out of the church, followed by Estelle and a tiny Robbie, in the arms of the gallant William Warfield.

There were other backstage dramas that ended not in marriage but in angry outbursts—many of these triggered by cast members who were outraged with having to share a dressing room with, as one upset party put it, "You selfish, son-of-a-bitch, pain-in-the-ass, never-spring-for-a-fucking-box-of-Kleenex, no-talent phony!" I don't remember what the pairings were and what other major bones of contention there were, but among the warring roommates were:

Buddy Hackett, an extraordinarily creative and bright comedian who was as unpredictable and volatile as he was creative; Alan Dreeben, (a.k.a. Alan Dexter), a lover of automobiles (the classic Duesenberg in particular), and one of the most brilliant and unsung comedy talents ever; Howard Morris, an army buddy with whom I had worked at the NYA Radio Workshop, and later on *Your Show of Shows,* was now caught in the backstage crossfire, and I felt that the least I could do for an old friend was offer him a safe haven in my dressing room; and William Le Massena, a gentleman, a classically trained actor, and possessor of a deep, booming voice, which he used effectively to rail at his "slovenly, thoughtless, self-centered bastard" of a roommate.

Starting in the second month of our Chicago run, I had a steady stream of disgruntled boarders sharing my cramped dressing room. I'm not quite sure of the order, but I remember Buddy Hackett stomping in, carrying all of his costumes rolled up in a ball.   •

"I can't take it up there with that fuckin' shithead!" he announced, tossing his costumes on the floor. "Can I change in here for a while, just until I kill him?" Buddy let the shithead live, and soon returned to his dressing room.

Alan Dreeben was my roommate for the longest spell and, at one time, I believe I had two squatters sharing my space and venting their spleen. Since I was the only member of the company who had a baby, I think they looked upon me as a father figure. There was no denying that, at twenty-five, I had inadvertently become a stabilizing influence in the company and, as it turned out, this was not a bad thing to be.

Alan Dreeben was the only member of the company to own a car. When he learned we would be in Chicago for six months, he ran out and bought a shiny, good-as-new second-hand, six-hundred-dollar Ford. He loved that six-cylinder sedan and treated it with the care and respect he would a Duesenburg. He told us each day where he had driven "her" and how that "little beauty purred" when he opened her up on Lake Shore Drive. One matinee, Alan, who was in my dressing room putting on his makeup, was called to the back-stage pay phone. I was coming up the alley to the stage door when I heard some madman cursing the "sick damned world" and the "dirty rotten bastard sonofabitch bastard bastard" who "should be arrested, shot, and kicked in the balls!" A moment later I heard the madman groaning and straining, and then a strange splintering sound, as if something was ripped from a wall. I learned, when a big block of metal came bouncing its way toward me, that Alan had torn an entire phone box from its mooring and shot-putted it in my direction. I managed to avoid getting hit, but I was unnerved. Alan had learned from his wife, Betty, that some kid, firing a BB gun, had made a small hole in his beloved car's windshield! Alan continued to scream about this "sick, fucking vandal" and stopped only when I reminded him that we had a show to do. It was after the "flying phone missile" incident that I composed the following letter.

July 15, 1947

Dear Mr. Levin,

Neither for my good reviews in Boston, Buffalo, Toronto, Cleveland, and Detroit, nor for the sensational review I received from Claudia Cassidy am I asking you to reconsider my position. I would never ask you to give me a raise for doing the job I contracted to do, but I am for a job that was not covered in our original deal—a job that has been thrust upon me by circumstance. I trust that our company manager, Max Gendel, has kept you abreast of what has been going on backstage for the past couple of months.

For my noncontracted work as the company psychiatrist, I ask you now to consider some appropriate compensation.

Very truly yours,
Carl Reiner

Two days later, I received Mr. Levin's response.

Dear Carl,

For rendering services not covered in original contract we are adding thirty-five dollars a week to your current salary.

> Best regards,
> Herman

I like to think that my brilliant and attractive daughter, Annie's, becoming an eminently successful psychotherapist is in small part attributable to a psychology gene she inherited from me, but, on reflection, she is more likely to have inherited that talent from her mother.

The summer of '47 was insufferably hot. Our room at the New Lawrence Hotel was not air-conditioned, and all we could do was swelter and curse. One sleepless night, in a desperate attempt to find relief, I stuffed our bedsheets and pillowcases into the small refrigerator and let them chill for ten minutes, and it worked! The sheets got ten minutes of relief, but the moment we unfurled them in the hot air, they lost their chill. Yet another creative idea gone awry.

All things considered, the six months we spent in Chicago were among the most memorable and confidence building of my young theatrical life. We were sad and happy to be leaving Chicago. Sad to leave a town that made us feel welcome and sad that the show would be closing after we played two weeks in Los Angeles and two in San Francisco, but happy to be going to the West Coast, to Hollywood, where great things could happen to further our careers. It was not lost on any of us that Jules Munshin and Betty Garrett had been plucked from the Broadway cast and signed to MGM film contracts.

The train ride to Los Angeles was another experience I cherish. My last long train ride had been completely uncherishable. It was on a rattling troop train where I and fifty other soldiers, who slept in double-decker beds, reacted violently to the tainted beans served at dinner, and all got the midnight runs.

In contrast to that wartime nightmare, here I was with deluxe accommodations and great company. A private room, a wife and a six-month-old baby, who was adorable and adored by his parents and the entire cast. Howie Morris, Bob Fosse, Marian Niles, and Biff Liff kitchy-cooed the heck out of Robbie, as did most of the chorus girls, who fought for the opportunity to baby-sit him. Robbie spent most of the trip sitting on some pretty girl's lap, hypnotized by the moving panorama of America that passed outside the train window. He had just learned to crawl and spent a good deal of time wiggling his way up and down the aisles. To this day, I believe that Rob's healthy immune system is due to his having introduced bacterial-fighting antibodies into his system by stuffing old cigarette butts and chewing gum wrappers into his mouth. Actually, he did this just the one time. After that, his crawling was monitored by caring, guilt-ridden parents.

In Los Angeles, we checked into the Hotel Figueroa, which was walking distance to the Biltmore Theater. It was now a year and a half since the original show opened, and audience interest in sketches and songs about servicemen returning home was waning. We didn't feel any pressure about doing anything more on opening night than just giving it our best. I recall Alan Dreeben reading aloud bogus newspaper articles, in which he described the excitement and interest Daryl

Zanuck, Sam Goldwyn, and Louis B. Mayer had in coming to the show, hoping to find another Judy Garland, Gene Kelly or Danny Kaye. Little did we know how prophetic he was.

The reaction from the Los Angeles theatergoers was all we could ask for. The laughs were big, the applause was sustained, the curtain calls were unforced. I went home feeling that I had done well. Until after I visited the West Coast MCA office and met the agent who had been assigned to represent me, I had no idea *how* well I had done. My new representative was very young, and agent-style overcomplimentary, promising to investigate possible film work for me. I left feeling pleased that someone, even though he looked to be sixteen years old, was interested in my future.

As I walked into the basement garage to retrieve my rental car, a parking attendant poked his head out of a booth and asked if I was Carl Reiner. When I told him I was, he said, "Phone call!"

It was my wife. She had called my agent, who transferred the call to the garage.

"Honey, get to a radio as fast as you can," she ordered, "tune in five-seventy! Someone from the station called and said that George Fisher is coming on the air in sixty seconds to talk about the show!"

I had no idea who George Fisher was, but I knew I couldn't get to my car radio in time, so I asked the attendant if I could change the station on his radio. He was happy to oblige. I heard a man announce himself as "George Fisher, Your Hollywood Correspondent" and go on to say that he and motion picture producer George Jessel had attended the exciting opening night of *Call Me Mister.* He then proceeded to give me the kind of review that I still find too embarrassing to repeat. Even my dear mother would have questioned whether or not

I was being too highly praised. It far outdid the review I got from Claudia Cassidy. Mr. Fisher gave me the kind of hosannas that Einstein might have gotten had he chosen to go into comedy. He ended his review by spelling my name slowly and then, with great urgency in his voice, he shouted: *"Mr. Reiner, if you are listening to this program, please pick up a phone and call George Jessel at Twentieth Century Fox immediately! Sitting on Mr. Jessel's desk, there is . . . A BIG, FAT MOVIE CONTRACT, WAITING FOR YOUR SIGNATURE!"*

And then to make sure I heard it, he repeated that information, told us again he was George Fisher, and signed off.

I was trembling! The parking attendant invited me to use his phone. I got the studio's number from information and called George Jessel. "Georgie" Jessel! The former vaudeville comedian, the original star of the Broadway play *The Jazz Singer,* Toastmaster General of the United States, eminent eulogist, personal friend of Daryl F. Zanuck, and now working as a film producer for Mr. Zanuck. I thought, *It's like in the movies!*

His secretary, expecting my call, put me right through. Here now is a close-to-verbatim conversation I had with the man who had a "big fat contract sitting on his desk waiting for my signature."

"Mr. Jessel, this is Carl Reiner, I heard George Fisher's radio program and he said—"

"Yes, I know!" he said, quickly, "I'm glad you called. Carl, you were very good last night. Look, I don't want to make a tsimmes (a complicated Jewish dish made with carrots and prunes), but I'd like to see you at my office this afternoon, if you can make it."

I made it! It was my first visit to a movie studio and my first meeting with a movie producer, and was I ever impressed.

"Mr. Jessel is expecting you." a secretary said, pleasantly. "He'll be with you shortly."

I could not believe this was happening. I had started to worry about my future and wondered if I'd ever get another job. For eleven months I had not received one offer, and I began to think what insecure actors often think: "My career is over!" Now, sitting in George Jessel's outer office, a small jolt of self-confidence returned, along with a weird premonition that a job offer was imminent.

I was smiling dreamily when a short, middle-aged, dapperly dressed, neatly toupeed George Jessel breezed into the waiting room, handed his secretary a note, rattled off a string of instructions and, without ever glancing at me, reached down, squeezed my arm, and said, "Be with you in a minute, kid." He then walked to his office door, stopped, reminded his secretary to check his lunch reservation, kissed the tip of his middle and index fingers, touched them to the mezuzah on the doorframe and, without looking at me, said, "Carl, give it a kiss and come into my office!" I did as I was told.

Mr. Jessel's office was large, well-appointed, and looked like all the big producers' offices I had seen in movies. Before offering me a seat, Mr. Jessel took me for a guided tour of his walls, on which hung framed photographs of Mr. Jessel in the company of presidents, vice presidents, generals, admirals, senators, governors, and every movie star or celebrity worth draping an arm around. He ended the tour by reaching into his desk and pulling out an eight-by-ten glossy of him and Lana Turner. She was wearing a revealing white, skin-hugging satin gown.

"Would you like have this?" he asked as he started to sign it. "You spell your name with a *C*, don't you?"

I nodded yes to both questions. He handed me the photo,

then snatched it from me and with his pen drew a little cross on each of her nipples.

"Just calling your attention to Lana's first-rate bosom!"

With that, he settled himself behind a gigantic, highly polished desk and invited me to sit in a club chair opposite him. He offered me a foot-long cigar, which I declined. While he was lighting his, I glanced at his desk to see if my "big fat contract" was lying atop it, as George Fisher said it would be. It wasn't atop it as far as I could see, but it might have been in a drawer or under a stack of papers.

"So, Carl," he said, officially opening the meeting, "I sat in the first row last night—did you see me there? The hell with the small talk. You were terrific and so was the show. I predict that you're going to have a big career . . . and what I'd like to propose to you is—"

The phone rang and he picked it up, listened for a moment, sighed wearily and said, "Put him on! Overseas call," he explained to me. "I'm executive-producing this movie in Paris and the producer and director call me every other minute to solve problems they should be solving. They can't make a decision on their own. Hello? . . . Yes, I just told you to put him on."

"The director is a real shmuck!" Mr. Jessel informed me. "Hello, Buddy, what's the problem? I see . . . well, I can't help you unless I know what they are. . . . All right, read them to me."

Mr. Jessel listened impatiently, looked over at me, and shook his head. "All right, all right, calm down. I'll tell you what you do . . . shoot them both! . . . That's right, shoot them both! . . . You're welcome."

He hung up the phone hard and took a deep breath. "They've written two endings for the film, and they can't decide which one to shoot, so they call me from Paris. *Me, I* have to make the decision. I told them to shoot both endings. Those idiots can't make a decision without me. I don't know what the hell I'm paying them for."

Mr. Jessel flipped on the intercom, and barked, "Honey, hold my calls! I do not want to be interrupted."

He then turned his attention to me. Sighing the sigh of a man who carries all the world's burdens on his shoulders, he asked, "Now, what was I saying?"

I started to tell him that he was proposing something to me, when the phone rang again. He picked it up angrily, started to berate his secretary but stopped abruptly and stared at me while continuing on the phone, "Yes, yes, I want to talk to him."

"Sorry, Carl, but this is an important call," he explained, "for both of us. It's our casting director."

His eyes were locked on me as he acknowledged the voice on the phone. I have never been privy to a more exciting one-sided phone call.

"Yes, yes, I know the role," Mr. Jessel said, studying my face, "and I know the type you're looking for. . . . You're not going to believe this, but that actor is sitting in my office right now, not ten feet away from me, and I guarantee, he will knock shit out of the part. . . . Reiner, Carl Reiner . . . Yeah, it opened last night . . . he was great . . . Just a minute, I'll ask him."

Mr. Jessel turned to me and, very matter-of-factly, asked what my schedule was. I told him, and he relayed it to the casting director.

"He wants to know when you close in Frisco?"

"In four weeks," I answered.

"Four weeks," Mr. Jessel relayed.

George Jessel listened intently to his casting director, shook his head, and said, "Are you sure . . . because this Reiner kid would have knocked shit out of the part."

The two heartbreaking operative words in that sentence, "would have," rang in my head as I watched Georgie Jessel hang up the phone. I thought, *Would have knocked shit out of what part?* I never did find out.

"Too bad, kid," Mr. Jessel said, coming around from behind his desk, "but they're shooting your scene while you're in Frisco."

"My scene?"

"The one you would have been great in. Those are the breaks! Here," he said, handing me the autographed photo of him and Lana, "don't forget your picture!"

He put his arm around my shoulder as he escorted me to the door.

"You're a very talented kid, and there'll be other films and other parts," he assured me as he shook my hand. "We'll be talking soon, you can bet on it!"

I'm glad I did not bet on it, because it was twenty years before we talked again. I was at a Writer's Guild dinner where he shook my hand, and said, "I'm very pleased to meet you! Love your work, Paul."

If Georgie Jessel had not lured me to his office with the big-fat-contract-on-my-desk bait to publicize his position as an important executive at Twentieth Century Fox, I would have missed out on having "My First Hollywood Heartbreak" as a symmetrically satisfying ending to "My First Best Job."

4

ＡＳｔｒｏｋｅ ｏｆ Ｎａïｖｅｔé

(A SHORT TALE OF SHMUCKERY)

I am not sure that there is such a word as shmuckery, *but if there isn't, I will be happy to contribute it to Messers Funk or Wagnall or whoever is in charge of dubious acquisitions for their dictionary's next edition. Shmuck is Yiddish slang for "penis" and is used in impolite society to designate someone who does nincompoopy things. For a good part of my life, I have been an active member of that discipline.*

I was eighteen years old when I was offered what I consider to be my first well-paying, professional job in the theater. For an eight-week tour of Southern Colleges and High Schools as a member of The Avon Shakespearean Repertory Company, I was to be paid *thirty dollars a week!*

I traveled by bus to Atlanta, Georgia, the farthest I had ever ventured from my parent's Bronx apartment at 2089 Arthur Avenue. It was the first time I had seen For White Only and For Colored Only signs on drinking fountains and public toilets. I had heard about their existence but actually seeing the signs and watching people heed them was very unsettling. I encountered many eye-opening and eye-blinking experiences in my eight weeks traveling through the deep South, but I will not cite examples of the old South's demeaning and bigoted practices of legal shmuckery, but I will recall for you a tale of my own personal shmuckery. The passage of the Civil Rights Bill in 1964 helped the South to rid itself of its shmuckerian ways, but I, sad to say, from time to time, still struggle with mine.

Our first day of rehearsal for *As You Like It*, being held in the ballroom of the Hotel Tallulah in Atlanta, was most exciting. I had just finished auditioning for the role of Orlando in *As You Like It* and was rather pleased with myself. I didn't quite understand everything I was saying, but I said it all with conviction, a strong voice, and a slight Errol Flynnish English accent. During a break, the managing director of the company, Frank Selman, beckoned me to him. I had never met him. His younger brother, Harold, who was in his fifties, had been my contact with the company and was directing the rehearsal. Until the elder Selman had elected to retire a year or so earlier, he had been the star of this company. He was a most impressive man, radiating the air of a great actor. Walking with the aid of a cane, he slowly made his way to me. He seemed to be smiling, but as he approached it became clear that he was scowling. I concluded that he probably could see that I was a fake and was coming to fire me.

Mr. Selman brought his aquiline nose close to my less aquiline one, scanned my face, and instead of saying "Get off this stage with your phony accent," said, with an absolutely beautiful timbre in his voice, "Say after me!"

He delivered this as Boris Karloff might have, with an English accent and a slight lisp. "Thay afther me!" is what I heard.

Frank Selman then spoke the following from what I later learned was *Richard the Third.* His voice boomed, spittle sprayed from his mouth—his right hand trembled as he slowly raised it. The louder he spoke, the more spittle he sprayed, the weirder he looked—one cheek going limp, one eye drooping, his contorted lips and mouth struggling to deliver these words. "Now—ith—the winter of our—dith-contentt," he declaimed, "may—gloriuthh-ttthummer—by the thhun—of—yawwwwk. . . ."

Mr. Selman stopped and said quietly, "Thay!"

I assumed two things: that Mr. Selman wanted me to "thay" what he had just said and wanted me to say it exactly as he had said it. I reasoned that his performance, with his face taking on a gargoyle's look, was planned—he was depicting a character who was ugly and crippled. In my mind's eye, I saw Quasimodo, replete with the hump on his back and the face Charles Laughton affected in *The Hunchback of Notre Dame.* It made great sense to me.

I, who take pride in being a fair impressionist, outdid myself. I channeled Mr. Selman and impersonated his voice, his grimaces, and his pantomime to perfection, palsied hand and all. My lisping on the words, "discontent," "glorious," "summer" and "son of York," even to the volume of spit, was identical to his. When I finished declaiming "may gloriuthh thhhummer by the thhhhun of yawwwwk," an eerie silence descended in the room. The dozen or so actors who had witnessed my "audition" were all staring at me. Mr. Selman, too, was staring at me with his good eye, the eyebrow above it fully arched.

After trying to determine whether I was a complete idiot or

just an actor who follows directions too well, Mr. Selman smiled crookedly, and said, "Very good, young man, very good indeed."

The most astonishing aspect of this incident was that I was blithely unaware of what I had done, until a fellow actor, Gene Lyons, who would become a close and dear friend, came up to me, and asked, "Hey, what the hell were you doing?"

"I was doing what he told me to do, why?"

"Mr. Selman told you to make fun of his stroke?"

I could not make Gene or anyone believe that I was not aware that our boss had suffered a major stroke. How could I notice anything about the old man when I was so busy worrying about what he was noticing about me?

I went on to play Orlando and four other good roles in three other Shakespeare plays. I finally got comfortable enough with myself to notice many wonderful things and had the most treasured experience of my life to that date.

Now, with your kind indulgence, an afterthought. I might not have written the above anecdote were it not for my friend, Mel Brooks, who at a dinner party at Alan and Arlene Alda's home asked me if I were going to include my "making fun of a man with a stroke story" in this collection. I said that I was not intending to, because it needed to be performed. I did not think I could write it as effectively as I tell it. I told it that night for the benefit of Peter Jennings, who was the only guest at the small dinner party who had never heard the story. Everybody laughed, even my friends who had previously heard it.

Later that evening, Mel insisted that I try to make it work on paper. The following day, my manager, George Shapiro, offered the same advice. Since neither Mel nor George had ever steered me too wrong, I agreed to give it a try.

If, dear reader, you and I should ever cross paths or bump fenders, ask me to relate this story to you, and then tell me how well, or if, I succeeded.

5

ℒovely ℒegs

(A SECOND SHORT TALE OF SHMUCKERY)

For my second short tale, I must take you back with me to Washington, D.C., the city to which the army chose to send me in 1943. For some reason, the army thought that if I studied French at Georgetown University for nine months I would be qualified to go to France and be a French language interpreter for our American officers, who were desperate to know what their French counterparts were saying to them. I did learn how to speak the language well enough to order food in French restaurants and understand French films without reading every English subtitle.

After graduating from Georgetown, our company of French interpreters were shipped to Hawaii, and the company of graduating Japanese interpreters were sent to Paris. We were totally confused by the logic of those assignments, but who's to argue with the results? We won the war. "Confuse and conquer!" might have been our strategy.

While at Georgetown, when I wasn't in class struggling to master the more difficult tenses of the verbs and learning how to ask a French girl if she wanted to go to bed with me, my good buddy, Sol Pomerantz, and I would go into town on our days off and visit the local USO canteen to see a variety show or participate in one. After a year at the Gilmore Theater in New York, two years at the Rochester Summer Theater, performing roles in twenty-six plays, and a season touring with the Avon Shakespearean Company, I never lost the urge to get up on a raised platform and show off. To that end, I had worked up a comedy act that was good enough to get me invited to perform at the canteen. This was to be my second appearance there. I had not too long before plied my craft at Georgetown, having produced a Christmas show in which I did a monologue and a too-accurate impression of the dean of Foreign Services, Father Edmond Walsh, and the other good Jesuit fathers who taught various subjects in the School of Foreign Service. For that performance, I received the best audience reaction of my career and a serious request from Father Walsh never to do another performance like it. Since Georgetown was no longer an outlet for the ham within me, I was grateful to have the USO.

As I came through the USO foyer that led to the canteen ballroom, I spied a comely young lass seated on a white wicker settee, and she was smiling—at me. Since the dance portion of the evening had just ended, I assumed that the attractive girl had been dancing and was taking a breather before going back in to see the show. Her smile broadened as I approached her, and I smiled back. I had not intended to stop but did when I heard a melodious "Hello, there!"

"Hello," I sang back.

"Are you going to perform again this evening?"

"I am," I said, enjoying her smile. "Were you here last week?"

"I was. You were so funny." She giggled. "I hadn't intended to come tonight, and I'm glad I did."

"I hope I don't disappoint you. I'm trying some new things. Well, nice talking to you," I said, starting off.

"Don't you remember me?" she asked brightly.

"I'm sorry," I said, "did we meet before?"

"Well, not formally," she said, coyly, "but we did share a few moments together."

Not possible, I thought. If I had shared anything with this pretty girl, I would remember. I decided to white-lie myself out of the situation.

"Let me look at you," I said mock seriously, looking her over from head to toe, pausing to stare at her lovely legs, which were daintily crossed at the ankles. "Of course, I remember you. Now that I see those pretty legs. I'd never forget legs like yours!"

I had made a bad joke, paraphrasing the cliché, "I never forget a face!" but the young lady found it funny and chuckled. It was an honest flirt, because I *have* always appreciated women's legs.

During my turn onstage, I looked about to see if my leggy girl was laughing, but I couldn't find her. As I ended my program, I spotted her at the back of the hall and caught a glimpse of her lovely legs. My heart leaped, or I should say, fell! I was right about *one* of her legs, it was perfection, but the other was polio stricken, supported by a metal brace. I didn't know what to do or say. What do you say to someone whom you have, inadvertently or not, offended? "How could I ever forget legs like yours?!" Damn!

While accepting compliments from some soldiers, I was thinking, *How can I face this girl? What do I say to her? Do I have to face this girl? Do I have to say anything? Is there a back door I can scoot out of? Am I a shit?* I decided I wasn't one and raced to the foyer, not sure she would be there—or whether or not I wanted her to be there. She was there, seated on the settee, and, without asking her permission, I sat down next to her.

"You were wonderful!" she said. "Your new jokes were funny."

"Thank you. Some of the ones I did onstage were pretty good," I heard myself say, "but the one I made to you about your legs was god-awful, and I apologize."

The part of my psyche that controls assuaging of guilt and the reclamation of mental comfort put those words in my mouth. Whichever prophet said, "The truth will set you free" was one smart prophet. That young lady, who had lived with her problem since she was a child, immediately put me at ease by telling me that she knew I was not aware of her condition and admitted to enjoying the compliment her good leg received.

"Well, let's see, now," she said, proudly, showing it off to its best advantage by extending it and pointing her toe. "It *is* a pretty nice-looking leg, as legs go."

Had I not been committed to a Bronx lass I had met a year earlier, who also had great legs, who knows what might have developed. I remember sitting and chatting with her for a long time and being openly flirtatious. I meant to reaffirm something she probably already knew, that she was a most attractive and desirable young woman.

I do not remember her name, but I would love to know that she had a good life. I feel that she did.

6

My Fifty Years with the 2,000 Year Old Man

When I met Mel Brooks in 1950, we were both working on the venerated television program, *Your Show of Shows*. I was a twenty-eight-year-old actor, and Mel, the youngest member of a brilliant writing staff, assumed he was twenty-four. Had I not watched a Sunday night television program, *We The People Speak*, Mel Brooks would never have discovered his true age.

We the People Speak was a weekly news program hosted by Dan Seymour. Each week, using actors to impersonate the people making the news, they would dramatize the important events of the week. What I heard one Sunday night was, I thought, appalling and begging to be satirized. It seemed like a perfect vehicle for Sid Caesar. I could not wait to discuss it with Sid, the writing staff, and Max Liebman, the boss of us all.

No one had seen the show, so that Monday, in Max's office, I did a re-creation of one of their re-creations of the news.

"Ladies and gentleman," I said, mimicking Dan Seymour's delivery, "the voice you are about to hear belongs to a plumber who was in Josef Stalin's toilet. While fixing a faucet in the washbasin, this is what the plumber overheard:

". . . and I hear Stalin say," I reported, using a Russian accent, " 've goink to blow up vorld Turrsday!' "

I know you are shaking your head, but I stand by that quote. Everyone in Max Liebman's office—Max, Sid Caesar, writers Lucille Kallen, Mel Brooks, and head writer Mel Tolkin—was sure that I had made it up. I remember saying that if Stalin actually said that, shouldn't Dan Seymour tell President Eisenhower or the Congress about it before scaring the crap out of everyone in America who owns a seven-inch, black-and-white television set? And then to illustrate how utterly ridiculous the whole premise was, I pointed to young Mel Brooks.

"Here with us today, ladies and gentlemen," I announced à la Dan Seymour, "is a man who was actually at the scene of the Crucifixion, two thousand years ago. Isn't that true, sir?"

Mel, aging before our eyes, sighed and allowed a sad "Oooooh, boy" to escape from the depths of his soul.

Here now is the moment Mel Brooks and the world discovered that a two-thousand-year-old man was living inside the body of a handsome, twenty-four-year-old comedy writer. I use the word *handsome* objectively. I know Mel will not be upset if, when writing about him, I stick to the truth.

I pressured the Old Man and asked, "You knew Jesus?"

"Jesus . . . yes, yes," he said, straining to remember, "thin lad . . . wore sandals . . . always walked around with twelve other guys . . . yes, yes, they used to come into the store a lot . . . never bought anything . . . they came in for water . . . I gave it to them . . . nice boys, well-behaved. . . ."

For a good part of an hour Mel had us all laughing and appreciating his total recall of life in the year 1 A.D. I called upon Mel that morning because I knew that one of the characters in his comedy arsenal would emerge. The one that did was similar to one he did whenever he felt we needed a laugh break. It was a Yiddish pirate captain who had an accent not unlike the 2,000 Year Old Man.

"I'm stuck in port," the pirate captain would complain, "I can't afford to set sail. Do you know much they're asking for a yard of sail cloth? It doesn't pay to plunder anymore!"

Starting that day in Max's office, and continuing for ten years, I would ask Mel to channel the Old Man, and he would oblige by telling us things that made us laugh and, later, our wives, when we came home and repeated "what Mel said" that day. The Old Man became so popular that dinners in diverse places like New Rochelle and Fire Island would be built around the Old Man's availability. The most successful dinner parties we have ever given or attended were the ones Mel Brooks attended and shared his firsthand knowledge of all the important people and events of the last five millennia. Yes, I did say five millennia. I know I am opening up a can of caponata by suggesting that the Old Man may be a good deal older than two-thousand because of his firsthand knowledge of Moses and Phil, who was thought to be the deity before being killed by a lightning bolt. No one till now has ever questioned his age, and I'm sorry for bringing it up, but it has troubled me. It could well be that vanity keeps him from admitting that he is three millennia older than he claims to be. I must ask him the next time I interview him.

This much we do know: Between 1950 and 1960, the 2,000 Year Old Man was, to quote Mel Brooks in one of his other incarnations, Dr. Holldanish, when asked if he was well known, replied, "I am *very* well known to those who *know* me and completely *unknown* to those who have never heard of me."

Such was the case with the 2,000 Year Old Man. Among an elite circle of friends who enjoyed laughing until their sides hurt and nausea overtook them, the Old Man was completely *known* and the most sought-after dinner invitee on both coasts. Since I was concerned that my probing questions and Mel's brilliant ad-lib answers might be lost to posterity, I bought a portable Revere, a reel-to-reel tape recorder, and taped all of our sessions.

Along with my recordings, Mike Elliot, a Fire Island friend who had a professional recording set-up in his home, presented me with copies of the dozens of sessions he recorded. What a summer! Free Saturday night dinners and free tapes for my archives. In those archives are hundreds of examples of Mel's brilliance. I hope someday to remember where I stored them. They could be worth thousands of dollars or billions, depending on the state of the economy.

It was at one of these Fire Island soirees that Joe Fields heard Mel holding forth and became our number one benefactor. Joe Fields, Broadway producer and co-author of Broadway musicals and plays like *Wonderful Town* and *Dear Ruth*, arranged a dinner party in New York and invited Mel and Estelle and me to attend. It was held at the home of Broadway producer, songwriter, owner of Billy Rose's Aquacade and newspaper columnist, Billy Rose. It was a little nervous making seeing the guest roster and realizing that we're about to do a command performance for Broadway royalty. There we were, after dinner, performing for the likes of Lerner and Loewe, the geniuses who created the music and lyrics for *My Fair Lady, Brigadoon,* and *Camelot,* and Harold Rome, the composer-lyricist of *Pins and Needles, Fanny, Wish You Were Here* and *Call Me Mister*. Mel and the Old Man, as expected, convulsed Billy Rose and the members of his royal court.

At this point Mel Brooks had not yet met and swept Anne Bancroft off her feet, and was years away from writing and directing his first film, *The Producers,* and four decades away from becoming the reigning King of Broadway, by adapting his film into the super hit musical, *The Producers.* He was still defined by his ability to write fine monologues and sketches for *Your Show of Shows, Caesar's Hour,* and for *New Faces of 1952.*

During the ten years Mel and I had performed at people's homes, we were continuously asked why we had not made an album of this hilarious stuff.

A word now about why we held firm about not commercializing the 2,000 Year Old Man.

In the 1920s and '30s, there were wonderful comedians and comediennes whose material and performances were enhanced by their speaking with a Yiddish accent. In vaudeville there was Smith and Dale; in burlesque Eugene and Willy Howard; on Broadway Weber and Fields and Fannie Brice, (a star of the Zeigfeld Follies); on radio Mr. Kitzel, and a Mr. Shlepperman on *The Jack Benny Show*; Bert Gordon (the Mad Russian) on the *Eddie Cantor Show*; Mrs. Nussbaum on the *Fred Allen Show*; and Gertrude Berg and Eli Mintz on *The Rise of the Goldbergs*. The Yiddish accents they employed were all reminiscent of how Middle and Eastern European Jewish immigrants spoke English. Their accents were considered to be cute, charming, and funny, but when Adolf Hitler came along and decreed that all Jews were dirty, vile, dangerous, subhuman animals and must be put to death, Jewish and non-Jewish writers, producers, and performers started to question the Yiddish accent's acceptability as a tool of comedy. The accent had a self-deprecating and demeaning quality that gave aid and comfort to the Nazis, who were quite capable of demeaning and deprecating Jews without our help. From 1941 on, the Yiddish accent was slowly, and for the most part, voluntarily, phased out of show business.

Growing up in Brooklyn and listening to his uncles, his neighbors, and the shopkeepers talk and argue, Mel, blessed with a good ear for music, had no difficulty absorbing the lilting, Middle European Yiddish accent. Mel and I were very aware that our friends and fans were, for the most part, Jewish, and if they were not, they laughed and behaved as if they were. We were also under the impression that only New Yorkers or urban sophisticates would know what the Old Man was talking about or find it so funny that they would double over with laughter. Our audiences were always small, always select, and always happy to hear the Old Man tell intimate stories of his involvements with Joan of Arc, Helen of Troy, and Murray, the discoverer of ladies.

In 1960, the two things my wife and I missed most when we transplanted our family to California were our house on Fire Island and our friends in New York. In particular, I missed seeing Mel and interviewing his alter ego. By then Mel Brooks had written the book for two Broadway musicals, *Shinbone Alley* and *All American* (for details check Mel's book, due next fall). Every so often, Mel would make a trip to Los Angeles for meetings, about what, I don't know (check his book). On one of these trips, Joe Fields produced another lavish dinner party, this time at his own home. He made no pretense about the reason for the dinner party. He simply wanted to be the one who introduced his friends to "the funniest man in the world"!

In 1960, Joyce Haber, Hollywood's reigning gossip columnist, coined the phrase the *A-list party*. Well, this party had a lot of A's and A pluses. Wall-to-wall stars, whom I will bill in order of their appearance, or rather, in the order they appeared to compliment Mel and me after Mel had them falling off their plush seats for a good hour or more. Besides the 2,000 Year Old Man, I also interviewed Mel as a world-renowned artist and as an innovative psychiatrist.

In our ad-lib years, I always tried to surprise Mel by introducing him with a name and occupation he wasn't expecting. What is most amazing to me is that, if I said, "Here now is the world-renowned sculptor Sir Jacob Epstone," he would, without skipping a beat, create a whole new person, complete with voice, attitude, and an extraordinary knowledge of the subject's profession.

I have asked the 2,000 Year Old Man dozens of times to tell me which of his twelve hundred wives was his favorite and why she was. Each time he would say a different name and a give a different hilarious reason for favoring her. The wives whose names are known to us as his favorites, like Shirley and Zenobia, are just the names that popped out of his mouth when we recorded the albums. But I digress. (I will not digress again—unless a digression is in both our best interests.)

I would like now to return to my playwriting mode to re-create that most memorable and historic night for me, for Mel, and for his alter ego.

Time: *11:30 P.M., June 21, 1960*
Place: *A living room in a Beverly Hills mansion*
[Mel *accepting accolades,* Carl *accepting the overflow*]

[George Burns *approaches Brooks*
and Reiner]
GEORGE BURNS
[*puffing on an El Producto*]
Boys, very good—very funny . . . [*Exhales*]. Is
there an album?
MEL / CARL
No, there is no album. We only do it for
friends.

GEORGE
[*Puffs, exhales*]
If you don't put it in an album, I'll steal it . . .
I'm serious.
[*Takes a puff and exits*]
[Edward G. Robinson (*Little Caesar,*
Dr. Ehrlich's Magic Bullet, Double
Indemnity) approaches]
EDWARD G. ROBINSON
Fine work, fellers, fine work. It'd make a
dandy play. Write it up! I want to play that
thousand-year-old guy on Broadway. It could
be terrific. Write it!
[*Exits*]
[Steve Allen *walks over, hand extended,*
big smile on his face]
STEVE
Okay! Mel, Carl, I heard why you don't want
to do an album, but here's my proposition: I'll
pay for a studio, you go in and record your
stuff, edit it down, and if you don't like what
you hear, burn it. If you like it, I'll set you up
with a record company to distribute it.

MEL / CARL

You want to be our partner?

STEVE

No, it's all yours.

MEL / CARL

Why are you doing this?

STEVE

I love to see people laugh. Call me.

[*He exits*]

[*Crowd gathers around* Mel *and throws verbal bouquets at him, which he seems to enjoy catching*]

[Ross Hunter, *Universal Pictures producer of* Pillow Talk, Make Mine Mink, Flower Drum Song, Teacher's Pet, *and* Thoroughly Modern Millie, *etc. is chatting with* Carl Reiner]

ROSS HUNTER

You guys really cracked me up. Listen, Carl, do you have any interest in writing for films?

CARL

Well, I guess. . . . I've never written a screenplay.

ROSS HUNTER

Well, I know you can. The way you were interviewing Mel—you were creating a story with your questions.

I'm looking for a property for Doris Day. Do you have any ideas?

As a result of this party, the professional recording career of the 2,000 Year Old Man was launched, as was the screenwriting career of his Interviewer.

True to his word, dear, brilliant, Steve Allen arranged for us to record the 2,000 Year Old Man at World Pacific, a company that mainly produced jazz albums. The owner, Phil Turetsky, engineered and helped us edit the record. The session was recorded at his small studio into which a hundred or so family members and friends crammed themselves. We taped two hours of material that was ultimately edited down to forty-seven minutes. There was no script, no notes, and no guarantee that we would end up with an album. It hurt me to cut some of that material. To hear Mel searching for the vein of gold in each routine was, for me, as interesting and as exciting as the actual discovery. It could be likened to a trapeze artist who fails in his first attempt to do the triple-double and when he gets back up and nails it, the performer gets an even bigger ovation than he would have received had he succeeded that first time.

The album was well reviewed, but Mel and I still worried about its broad appeal. Half of the album was Mel performing many different characters. We were sure everyone would find them funny, but the title half was all the Jewish-accented Old Man. Would WASP America get him? Would Christians find the old Jew funny? Do "our people" still consider the Yiddish accent to be non grata? The highly successful appearances Myron Cohen made on the Ed Sullivan show spinning hilarious ethnic tales was a good indication that the Yiddish accent was again becoming grata.

Our unlikeliest fan, Cary Grant, gave us a hearty vote of confidence very early on. At the time of the release of the record, I was working for Universal Pictures writing the screenplay that Ross Hunter knew I had in me, *The Thrill of It All* for Doris Day and James Garner. Universal had given me a big, comfortable bungalow right next door to Cary Grant's bigger one. He popped in one day, introduced himself, which is something Cary Grant never need do. I immediately gushed like a teenager and told him how much I loved his work and a lot of other things he had heard too many times. As he was leaving, I presented him with a copy of our album and told him to "pop by anytime" . . . and darned if he didn't. He couldn't have been more effusive in his praise of Mel's 2,000 Year Old Man. He laughed as he repeated a line or two of the Old Man's dialogue, often answering "jaunty-jolly" when asked how he was feeling. He was so intrigued with the 2,000 Year Old Man that he suggested we do another album and include "a two-hour-old baby who can talk." On our second album there is a two-hour-old talking baby. Who is going to say no to Cary Grant?

When he left my office that day, he asked how he might get a dozen or so albums to give out to his friends. Naturally I was happy to have the albums delivered, complimentary of course, Cary Grant's favorite way to shop. Twenty years after leaving MGM, he still brought them his weekly laundry.

For the next few weeks, Cary would phone from time to time to report on the wonderful reactions he was getting from his friends, and add, "Ahh, Carl, would it be possible to get another dozen or so?" I was thrilled to oblige, and I was even more thrilled to hear that famous voice talking to me! The last call on this subject was the one that forever set to rest any concerns we had about our album. Prior to that last call, Cary had asked if he could have two dozen albums delivered to his office as he was flying to London for a few days and wanted to give them out to his British buddies. I did remark about the possibility of his buddies "not getting it" and he pooh-poohed my concern. "They do speak English," he reminded me.

A week later Cary Grant and I had this conversation.

CARY

Carl, the album was a smash! Everyone loved it!

CARL

Who is everyone?

CARY

Everyone one at the Palace.

CARL

Are you talking about Buckingham Palace?

CARY

Of course . . .

CARL

You . . . You played *The Two Thousand Year Old Man* at Buckingham Palace?!

CARY

Yes, and she loved it!

CARL

Who's she?

CARY

The queen. She roared.

This story and the dialogue, like 96 percent of this book, is absolutely true.

Well, there it was, the definitive word on the subject. Who is more non-Jewish, more Gentile, more WASP-like Christian, more 100 percent shiksa than the queen of England? Talk about broad appeal!

Not only was the album well received but it was nominated for a Grammy, which it didn't win. Because the Old Man and his Pesterer hung on and continued to record, their last effort, *The 2,000 Year Old Man in the Year 2000,* was awarded the Grammy that eluded them forty years earlier. I am hoping that after Mel Brooks helps to launch the planned ninety-four domestic and foreign productions of his phenomenal hit *The Producers* he will escort the Old Man to his neighborhood recording studio and let him go for a second Grammy.

As you may have gathered, I am very fond of Mel and his brain. On the lecture circuit, I borrow liberally from my friend's brain. I quote him often and to excellent effect. Until recently, I was certain that Mel had never quoted me or had a need to. However, a month or so ago, I called his home and got his answering machine. It was Mel's voice saying just three words, "Leave a message!" I was surprised—he had appropriated the message I had been using for years, which was, "*Please* leave a message." His was one word shorter than mine, and I think ruder, but the fact that he thought enough of my message to appropriate it, was for some reason strangely satisfying.

7

The Man with the Blue-Veined Cheek

(THE THIRD SHORT TALE OF SHMUCKERY)

I am happy to note that these doltish acts were committed in the first third of my life.

It was 1957, I owned an affordable home on Bonnie Meadow Road in New Rochelle, had a good marriage, good kids, and was gainfully employed. I was artistically content, having been twice awarded an Emmy for my Second Bananaring of television's greatest First Banana, Sid Caesar, and still capable of embarrassing myself.

After the dissolution of the ground breaking musical-variety show *Your Show of Shows*, Sid Caesar went out on his own. He had rented offices and rehearsal rooms in the Milgrim Building on West Fifty-seventh Street and invited me to be a part of his new show, *Caesar's Hour*. Besides being a second banana, I was also a trusted member of the creative team, which gave me access to Sid's ear into which I could whisper advice, opinions, and suggestions for where to eat lunch. Knowing of my innate charm and my enviable ability to bullshit with the very best in the field, Sid would often invite me to attend the goodwill-type meetings that sponsors and network heads request when everything is going very well or very badly. This meeting, I believe was the obligatory season-opening let's-see-if-we-can-get-those-ratings-up pep talk.

We all gathered in Sid's well-appointed office. I knew most of the network brass but none of the new sponsors or advertising people. After some preliminary introductions and the accompanying chitchat, one of the new team of admen, who was seated in a corner of the big leather couch, waved me over and invited me to join him. I will call this gentleman Ted, because that may have been his name.

Ted spoke enthusiastically about last year's shows and made complimentary references to a couple of my performances. Very soon after he started talking, I stopped listening and concentrated on trying to avoid looking at the left side of his face and forehead or acting as if I was not revolted by what I saw. I did all I could do to keep from grimacing, and told myself, *If he can go through life accepting this disfigurement, I should be able to spend a few minutes behaving civilly.*

As he talked, I kept thinking about the photos of fetuses I had seen in *Life* magazine, the translucent skin of the unborn baby's face and head, allowing for an intimate and disturbing view of the circulatory system with its patchwork of bluish veins and red capillaries. On the left side of Ted's face was a birthmark like none other I had ever seen—it covered most of his cheek and forehead.

Ted, a seemingly secure sort, obviously had come to terms with this thing and either chose not to have it cosmetically altered or knew it to be unalterable. It was thrice the size of the birthmark Gorbachev sported on his forehead. When I finally allowed myself more than a cursory glance, I saw what looked like a complex road map with finely etched blue-veined roads crisscrossing from just below his cheek to his forehead and ending at his hairline. It looked like a map of Connecticut, and I thought, *Connecticut? He's in advertising, half of the people in advertising live in Connecticut. Did he, when drunk one day, decide to have a map of his home state tattooed on his face?* Tattoo, birthmark, skin disease, or a genetic capillarial fragility, whatever it was, I could not look at it, and I hated myself for being so squeamish.

My role was to cater to bigwigs like Ted, so I hung in. And good old Ted, by turning out to be a man of rare taste and perception, was making it more and more difficult for me to leave. How can I walk away from a man who tells me what a huge fan I have in his wife and who seemed genuinely interested in hearing about my wife and kids and the dynamics of the family. While I was thinking all this, suddenly Ted jumped up.

"Would you like some Perrier?" he asked, "I'm getting one for myself."

While I was declining his offer, he was off to the drink and snack table. As he popped the top off a bottle of Perrier, Ted glanced up at the wall mirror behind the table and peered into it.

"What the fuck is that!?" he screamed, touching his face, "Hey, Carl, did I have this . . . thing . . . on my face while we were talking?"

I was tempted to say "What thing?" but I nodded.

"Why the hell didn't you say something," he asked, trying to rub out the map of Connecticut with his pocket hanky, "or are you in on a practical joke?"

I assured him that I was not and approached to get a better look at those blue veins which were now a messy, bluish purple smudge.

"So Ted," I asked, lightly, "what the devil is that ugly, blue mess on your face—that I barely noticed?"

Ted suddenly slapped himself hard on his forehead and recalled leaning his hand on a piece of carbon paper when talking to the receptionist. (Remember carbon paper?)

"And right after that, I made a phone call and rested my head in my hand. Just before you sat down," he said, clearing up the mystery, "I remember seeing this blue stuff on my hand and wiping it off on my hanky. But Carl, what the devil were you thinking when you looked at me? Why didn't tell me I looked like a prune?"

At this point I told Ted the story that I related to you earlier—"Lovely Legs"—and how, because of that embarrassment, I had vowed never to make reference to or joke about anyone's physical traits—except my own.*

———

*Bald-headed jokes! I wrote and encouraged other writers to write jokes about Alan Brady's baldness (my character on *The Dick Van Dyke Show*).

8

Off-Key—On-Key

There are certain memories I have of my early days on the legitimate stage and in television that are for the most part pleasant, but the painful memories are the ones that seem to bubble up more often. I was chatting with Sid Caesar the other day about the lovely reception the sketches of *Your Show of Shows* and *Caesar's Hour* were receiving from their airing on Public Television, and he reminded me of how, on *Caesar's Hour,* I once turned a golden moment into a leaden one.

Before I describe that embarassing moment, I'd like to go on record and say loudly that Sid Caesar is, in my estimation, the greatest sketch comedian who ever lived, bar none, double exclamation point!! A year before I became a member of his troupe, I watched and admired his work on *The Admiral Broadway Revue,* the precursor to *Your Show of Shows.* I remember saying to my wife, "That guy is sensational, he's doing the kind of comedy I love." I also remember thinking, *I belong on that show,* but did nothing to make that happen. I always wait for fate or a good agent to step in, and in this case it was Max Liebman, the producer of *The Admiral Broadway Revue.*

Max Liebman, mentor to Danny Kaye and Sid Caesar, was brought in to doctor a couple of the sick comedy sketches in *Alive and Kicking,* a new musical in which I had a part. It was playing Philadelphia, and on its way to Broadway. It got there but closed in six weeks. Dr. Liebman could not save the patient but he did save one of the cast members. He invited me to become Sid Caesar's straight man in a new show he was producing for NBC that fall.

As I think about it, the nine exciting years I spent with Sid on *Your Show of Shows* and *Caesar's Hour* were the result of being in a bad Broadway show at the right time.

Ah, yes, the leaden moment!

I am not being immodest when I say that I was gifted with a good operatic-type voice. I sported a three-octave range, could comfortably negotiate a high G, and on occasion, by risking a hernia, a high C. Along with my gift came my curse, the inability to sing on pitch and in rhythm. Being pitch and rhythm-challenged all but guaranteed that I would never fulfil my dream of being a leading tenor of the Metropolitan Opera, which I had planned to be when I first heard Enrico Caruso sing "*Vesti la giubba*" on my father's windup Victrola. That phonograph was a piece of furniture that stood four feet tall and was in use in our Bronx apartment for thirty years. For the first fifteen years it played my father's collection of Red Seal records of opera singers and violin soloists. For the remainder of its days, its record compartments served as a pantry to store cans of Heinz's soups and Bumble Bee salmon.

When called upon to lift my voice in song, I could manage, with proper rehearsal and serious concentration, an on-key, in-rhythm acceptable rendition of that song. Whenever improvising my own mock operatic aria or a phoney recitative, I rarely sang off-key, and if it was off, no one knew. It sounded as if I were mocking Arnold Schoenberg's *Sprech-stimme* (speaking voice) that the composer created for his off-key-sounding opus, *Pierrot Lunaire*. For my efforts, I got big laughs, unlike Schoenberg who had to settle for applause and immortality.

When I performed with Sid Caesar, Nanette Fabray, and Howard Morris in the opera burlesques that were featured on *Caesar's Hour*, I was able to use my dubious musical gift for fun and profit. Singing fake arias for millions of people was the closest I'd ever get to realizing my dream of becoming the next Caruso. In the four or five opera takeoffs we performed, I had managed to stay on-key, until that fateful night, when, in the last scene of our opera, *Cyranosa*, I lost my way! In a dueling scene, after being stabbed through my heart, the orchestra punctuated the thrust by playing a loud, dramatic chord which included my trusty high G, the note I would belt out and sustain fortissimo. The principals and chorus needed that key note to cue them into the rousing finale. Sid Caesar, who is a fine musician, voiced concern about my ability to pick my note out of the chord the orchestra would play as I was stabbed.

To allay his fears, I mentioned to Sid that in *Call Me Mister,* the conductor, Lehman Engel, who was privy to my musical shortcomings, solved the problem by arranging for a solo trumpet note to be played as I stepped out of the wings to start singing the opening song. For a year on the road and three months on Broadway, the opening number of *Call Me Mister*, thanks to that trumpet note, was on-key and in rhythm.

Sid reasoned that, if a single trumpet playing my note was a good idea, a better idea would be for the entire orchestra to play that note. To guarantee that I hit it, our conductor,

Bernie Green, arranged for every instrument to play the high G. Perfect scheme, almost perfectly executed. Here, now, is the sequence of events that permanently pasted this story into the scrapbook of my mind.

At the end of the dramatic scene, when Cyranosa thrusts his sword home, every instrument in the thirty-piece orchestra played the high G. Instead of belting out a G, I let out a skull-popping high C which caused Sid and the studio full of performers and musicians to shake their heads in unison and disbelief. It took more than a few bars for the singers to repair the musical mayhem by modulating to the original key, and singing an adrenalin-assisted, ultra-rousing finale.

It's been fifty years since we performed Cyranosa, but whenever Sid Caesar and I reminisce about that "good ol' day," invariably Sid will start to laugh and repeat what he said to me that night as we walked to our dressing rooms.

"Carl, I don't believe it! A whole, entire, high-priced orchestra with thirty-five professional musicians blast a G natural right at your head and you give 'em back a high C? How the hell did you do that?"

That night, I explained how, and I have explained it to him many times since then, and he still shakes his head, laughs, and asks again, "How the hell did you do that?"

Here is my side of the story:

A young, eager member of the chorus, a soprano, playing one of the townfolk, was standing a foot away from me and reacted to the stabbing by screaming directly into my left ear a bloodcurdling, brain-rattling, memory-destroying high C! It completely obliterated the high G the entire orchestra had just placed there.

Had I been born with the ability to retain that fateful G and been able to sing it out loudly and confidently, my life might have taken a different turn. I am pragmatic enough to know that I probably would not have reached the operatic heights of a Pavarotti, a Domingo, or even a Carrera, but I like to think that if those guys heard me sing "Rachel" from *La Juive* or "La donna è mobile" from *Rigoletto* they might consider renaming their group, "The *Four* Tenors!"

9

A Purse Is Not a Pocket Book

One very late evening in 1957, after my wife and children had gone to bed, I found myself in the den of our house in New Rochelle staring at a typewriter I had bought but never used. Since learning to type fourteen years earlier in an army teletype school, I had found no reason to type. Now on this lovely spring night I had found a reason. Actually two reasons, the first being an urge to discover how much of my touch-typing skills had eroded by disuse. The second reason concerns a vengeful trait in my personality that surfaces occasionally, a trait of which I am not proud. I promise to discuss it in an epilogue to this story.

I started that night by putting a new ribbon in my manual typewriter, rolling in a sheet of paper, and, without looking at the keys, speedily typing up the traditional practice sentence.

Noe is the tume for a goood men to come th e aife of thier pastry.

I was pleased to discover that I had lost little of my typing skills. After retyping the sentence a few times, my last effort showed a marked improvement.

Now is the time for all goodmem to comw to the aid of their paryt.

Two hours later, I had typed up a four-page short story about a senile but dogged old woman, who had worked hard for two days cooking an elaborate Friday dinner for her son and daughter-in-law, who do not show up because she had forgotten to invite them. That morning, without fanfare, I handed the story to my wife.

"Read this," I said, and went to the bathroom.

Ten minutes later, she called out, "Honey, this is a very touching story. Who wrote it?"

Estelle had given me my first literary review, and it encouraged me to write another story that night. This one, a five-pager, about a nine-year-old Little Leaguer and his boorish, loudmouthed father, who encourages his son, the pitcher, to "Hit him in the head! No more homers for this bum!"

In a couple of weeks, I had amassed about a dozen stories that my wife thought good enough to send out into the world. I asked my literate neighbor and friend, Julian Rochelle, a successful textile manufacturer, if he would read them and tell me what he thought. He thought my stories were delightful and asked if he could give them to a friend who he knew would enjoy them. He said that his friend "was in pocketbooks," but I didn't care who he gave them to. What tickled me was Julian putting my stories on his recommended reading list.

That Saturday night, Julian and his wife, Sylvia, had invited us to a buffet dinner. It was always a pleasure to see "dinner at the Rochelles" noted on our calendar—the food was always excellent and the wine and the conversation sparkling.

At this party there was an eclectic group of neighbors, theater folk, and associates of Julian's from the textile industry, many of whom we were meeting for the first time. A man, who I assumed was one of Julian's customers, sought me out to tell me that he admired my work on *Caesar's Hour* and enjoyed reading my short stories.

"I'd like to take you to lunch," he added, nonchalantly, "when you have some time."

"I'll check my calendar," I lied, pulling away. "Thanks for reading my stories."

I searched out my host, whom I found at the buffet table.

"Hey, Julian, what do I do about your friend?" I said, guiltily. "I'm happy that he liked my stories, but he wants me to have lunch with him. Authors don't have to go to lunch with everybody who likes their stories, do they? Probably wants to ask me what Sid Caesar is really like."

"Let him take you to lunch," Julian suggested, "it might be worthwhile."

"What'll he do? Give me a wholesale price on an alligator pocketbook?"

Julian laughed. I had assumed that Julian's friend bought fabrics from him to make linings for the pocketbooks he manufactured. When Julian mentioned on the phone that the man was in pocketbooks, I thought he was talking about the kind women sling over their shoulders, not the Pocket Books they read.

At our luncheon, Julian's friend told me that he had arranged for me to meet with Mr. Goodman, an editor at Simon & Schuster—"at my convenience"—which turned out to be right after lunch.

"So, Mr. Reiner, what would you like to do with these twelve short stories of yours?"

"Have them published. I had this idea. Paperback books sell for thirty-five cents a book. I thought I'd write thirty-five stories and title the book 'A Penny a Story'."

"It is a cute idea, but, traditionally, books of short stories don't sell as well as novels. Now, if you had a novel . . ."

"I don't."

"You could," he suggested, "if you took one of your short stories and expanded it. Think about it."

I did. What I thought about was "Fifteen Arthur Barringtons," one of my stories that might lend itself for novelizing. It dealt with the insecurity a young actor feels when competing with other actors for a part. Arthur Barrington, whom I described as resembling me at seventeen, wonders if any of the fourteen other handsomer, taller, blonder actors with great-sounding theatrical names who are waiting to audition had changed his name, as he had, from something like David Kokolowitz to a less Jewish-sounding one like Arthur Barrington. To fortify himself for the audition, he decides that all of them had changed their names.

Mr. Goodman agreed that the trials of an aspiring young actor was a worthy subject for a novel and suggested that I get started. I told him that I required one thing from Simon & Schuster that would facilitate my writing such a novel.

"And that would be?"

"Pressure! I work best under pressure—an early deadline would do it."

He was more than accommodating. He gave me a September 30 deadline *and a thousand dollar advance!* He had doubled the pressure on me, and I thanked him for doing so. The only element missing was the "how" as in "how the hell do you write a novel?"

There are many people who believe that there are certain coincidences in life that are supernaturally induced by some unknown cosmic force, but I firmly believe that a coincidence is a coincidence is a coincidence. I do appreciate the really strange ones in which I was a participant. There are others that I remember with awe and affection. (See Chapter 17, "Two Weird Coincidences.")

I am sure many of you will insist that the following coincidence was orchestrated by a divine intervener.

I came home from my meeting at the publishers without a clue as to how to start writing a novel and wondering if I had promised to do something I was incapable of doing. While thinking these negative thoughts as I got into bed that night, I casually picked up a book that had been lying on my night table for weeks. It was Fred Allen's *Much Ado about Me*. I loved Fred Allen and never missed his weekly radio show. After reading a short foreword that John Steinbeck had written, I jumped out of bed and started to pace. The great Fred Allen had faced the same dilemma I was facing and had told John Steinbeck that he had foolishly committed to writing his autobiography without having a clue in the world as to how to go about it. John Steinbeck gave him, and now me, not one but many clues. I had found my Rosetta stone!

Here now are Mr. Steinbeck's words of advice:

Don't start by trying to make the book chronological. Just take a period. Then try to remember it so clearly that you can see things: what colors and how warm or cold and how you got there. Then try to remember people. And then just tell what happened. It is important to tell what people looked like, how they walked, what they wore, what they ate. Put it all in. Don't try to organize it. And put in all the details you can remember. You will find that in a very short time things will begin coming back to you, things you thought you had forgotten. Do it for very short periods at first but kind of think of it when you aren't doing it. Don't think back over what you have done. Don't think of literary form. Let it get out as it wants to. Over tell it in the matter of detail—cutting comes later. The form will develop in the telling. Don't make the telling follow a form.

Sitting in the tiny den of our Fire Island beach house, balancing my portable Smith Corona typewriter on my lap, and armed with John Steinbeck's instructions, I started typing my book. I typed away for most of the day, every day while Robbie, Annie, and Estelle did what we always did for the six summers we had vacationed on the Island. There were a few writers on the island whom I made feel guilty by clacking away while the sun shone. Reggie Rose, the writer/creator of *The Defenders*, the television show that was the precursor of all of today's quality courtroom dramas, threw pebbles at my window every time he passed by—to let me know that I was disturbing his peace.

For six summers, while on thirteen-week hiatuses from *Your Show of Shows* and *Caesar's Hour*, I had lain on the beach, played in the sand with my kids, chatted with friends and neighbors at the local markets, dug for clams and enticed blue-clawed crabs out of the Great South Bay using a piece of string and a chicken neck. That summer, I was happy doing none of those things but worried that the thing I was doing was not worthy of being called a novel. My editor, Mr. Goodman, had called to say that he was in bed with a bad cold and available to read whatever I had written. I mailed out eighteen pages, and he called to say that I was on the right track and to continue. I continued until I had written 214 pages and was in the process of cleaning up the messy ones and doing final edits when I received a call from someone at Simon & Schuster informing me that Mr. Goodman had passed away. I could not believe it. The man was in his forties, and it was just inconceivable that anyone that young could just up and die. I had but that one conversation with him when he told me that I was on the right track. Now, not knowing if I had stayed on track, I buried my untitled book in a bureau drawer and went back to doing Fire Island things. I had finished the book weeks earlier than the September pressure date we had negotiated, but since Mr. Goodman was my only contact with his company, I assumed my project was canceled.

Two weeks after I had mourned the death of my editor and our project, I received a call from a Lee Wright, who informed me that she would be my new editor. Prior to her coming to the island to meet with me, she wanted to read what I had written. And what a good editor Lee Wright turned out to be! Not only did she give excellent lessons in grammar and punctuation, but she came up with the title for the book, *Enter Laughing*. I thought it was so perfect that I quickly added a humorous scene at the beginning of the book that accommodated her inspired title.

A week after this meeting, I slipped a spanking-clean copy of *Enter Laughing* into a manila envelope and headed to the harbor at Ocean Beach where I would board the *Fire Island Queen* and be ferried across the Great South Bay to the town of Bayshore, where I would retrieve my car (there are no cars allowed on Fire Island), drive to New York, and hand deliver my manuscript to my editor. On the ferry, I met a Fire Island neighbor and a fellow novelist, Herman Wouk.

"Hi, Carl," he said, "do you have a ride to New York?"

"Yes, thank you," I said, "I have a car."

"I don't. How would you like company?"

We had met at a couple of parties, and I liked and admired him and told him that I was honored to have him aboard.

The two-hour-plus drive to New York turned out to be the most uncomfortable and surreal driving experience I've ever had. When Herman Wouk settled into the passenger seat, I placed the manila envelope between us and started the car. The following is the conversation we had as I drove out of the parking lot.

HERMAN

What's in the manila envelope?

CARL

A little novel I've just finished writing. I'm delivering it to my publisher.

HERMAN

What are you calling it?

CARL

Enter Laughing.

HERMAN

Good title.

[*A long, long pause*]

Mind if I read it?

CARL

You want to read it now?

HERMAN

If you'd rather I not . . .

CARL

No, no . . .

While saying "No, no," I thought, *Reiner, are you really going to let this literary giant, who wrote* The Caine Mutiny *and* Marjorie Morningstar, *read your cockamamie novel? Are you nuts!?* I quickly decided that I was. I reasoned, *My cockamamie novel has humor in it, and this literary giant, before he became a literary giant, was a comedy writer on* The Fred Allen Show. Fred Allen?! Wow, another eerie coincidence!

CARL

I'd love you to read it, Herman.
[*Hands him the envelope*]
I wrote it to be read.

Herman Wouk took my life's entire literary output in his hands and started to read.

Herman was not aware that while he was reading *Enter Laughing* his life was in danger. My concentration was split between the road ahead and the book in his lap. I kept shifting my eyes from Herman's impassive face to the book, hoping to catch him smiling. What really irked me was hearing a snort or a chuckle coming from the "literary giant" and not knowing what scene or page he was reading when he made those sounds. The most upsetting thing of all was the speed with which he read my book. It took him just *two* hours to read what I had spent *two thousand* hours writing.

He was silent and pensive as he slipped the manuscript neatly back into the manila envelope. He paused much too long for my comfort before he turned to me.

HERMAN

[*A suggestion of a smile on his face*]
Very entertaining, Carl, very amusing.
CARL

Did you really like it?
HERMAN
Yes, I did. It has a lot of feeling. Good work.

CARL

Would you have said that if I hadn't given you
a free ride to New York?

HERMAN

Not likely.

[*His smile broadening*]

I wouldn't have read it.

Before dropping Herman Wouk off, he added a few complimentary things about my virgin effort and wished me luck.

Enter Laughing was published in 1958 and sold a few thousand copies in hardcover and a few thousand more in paperback. I presented a copy of the book to my friend and New Rochelle neighbor, Joe Stein, who paid me the ultimate compliment.

"This is a dandy book!" he said.

Some people might think that Joe's calling the book "dandy" was damning it with faint praise, but coupled with his saying that it would make "a dandy play" and actually adapting my novel into a "dandy hit" that ran on Broadway for more than a year I think qualifies the word as being a compliment of the first magnitude. Young, brilliant Alan Arkin playing the fictionalized version of me, made his Broadway debut in *Enter Laughing*, and went on to become one of America's most versatile and original actors. Joe and I later adapted the "dandy play" into a "dandy movie." Earlier, Joe had adapted a Sholem Aleichem story, "Tevya the Milkman" into the dandiest of musicals, *Fiddler on the Roof*.

Had it not been for Julian Rochelle's pocketbook/Pocket Book friend and the coincidental finding of Fred Allen's autobiography, I might not have written two more novels, a book of short stories, a children's book, and *The 2,000 Year Old Man in the Year 2000* (the book) that Mel Brooks and I "told to each other."

It frightens me to contemplate how bleak this world would be if those cherished works did not exist.

THE PROMISED EPILOGUE
Typing For Revenge

The driving force behind my need to type was born in the legendary writer's room of *Your Show of Shows*, where I made some contributions to the creative effort. I had been invited there by our producer, Max Liebman, and thought of myself as a writer without a portfolio. Sometimes I would come up with a less than brilliant idea or joke that would be summarily batted down by one or more of the staff. The one criticism that was the catalyst for my development came from the writer who reminded me, after dismissing my failed attempt to contribute, that I was "nothing but a fucking actor." To defend my name and the good name of all actors, I chose to use my typewriter as the weapon to bring down my detractor. I'd show the bastard! I'll dare to write something without asking for his approval. To his everlasting credit, the writer who reminded me that I was "nothing but a fucking actor" also said to me, after reading *Enter Laughing*, that I was "a fucking good writer."

To protect the identities of the other writers on the staff, who rarely used bad language, I will simply refer to my protagonist as Mel Tolkin, our head writer. Thanks, Tolk!

When I first accepted the thousand-dollar advance and realized that I owed somebody a novel, I told my wife that I couldn't possibly write a novel, because you need a lot of words to write a novel and I didn't have enough words or the erudition to do the job, and she said, "Honey, you've got something else—feelings."

With encouragement and advice from Steinbeck and Estelle, how could I miss?

10

This Is Your Lie, Carl Reiner

One of the best years of my life was 1960, and I didn't realize it until I started to write this chapter. For one, I had a good job cowriting the *Dinah Shore Show* every week and performing on it every other week.

Also in that year, my wife became pregnant with our third child. Our two older children, Robbie, who was born when I got the job in *Call Me Mister,* and Sylvia Anne Reiner, who dubbed herself "The Annie" when she was a tot, and has since dropped the "The," was conceived soon after I secured a role in the Broadway musical *Inside U.S.A.* It seems that conceiving children was a sure way for me to ensure getting a good job, and, also ensuring that there will be truly wonderful people in my life.

Robbie and Annie were thirteen and eleven respectively during my Dinah Shore days, and were doing well enough considering that their parents had uprooted them from their home in New Rochelle where their real friends lived. We did share a few good laughs with them, none more sustained and hearty than the one we had at the breakfast table, when I said, "Mom has a big surprise for you guys, guess what it is."

Their blue eyes lit up and big smiles erupted on their faces, just the reaction we had hoped for.

"A pony!" Annie screamed, "Mom, you're getting us a pony!"

"A pool table!" Robbie countered, equally excited, "You're getting a pool table!"

When we told them that Mom was going to have a baby, they exchanged quick glances, opened their mouths wide, and literally fell off their chairs. They laughed soundlessly as they rolled around on the floor. To avoid blacking out they inhaled short gulps of air that they quickly expelled, making loud, primitive snorts which made Estelle and me laugh. They were trying to say something, but it was unintelligible. Finally, with tears rolling down their faces, an apoplectic Annie pointed to her mother and blurted out, "*Mommy's . . . gonna . . . have a . . . p-pony!!*" A convulsed Robbie corrected, "*No, not a pony! . . . Mom's gonna have . . . a . . . pooool table!!*"

The image of their mother delivering either one of these cumbersome items they found hilarious. We did, too.

Back to the *Dinah Shore Show,* where I became party to the lie that triggered this confession. It all started a week earlier, when I did a mild comedy bit at the end of the show. Before throwing her famous good-night kiss to America, Dinah announced,

"And next week our *special* guest will be Gordon McCrea—and *our not-so-special* guest, Carl Reiner."

At this point, she acknowledged my presence in the audience and asked me to take a bow. The audience, heeding the blinking applause sign, applauded wildly, which I acknowledged by smiling and blowing kisses. Dinah thanked me and started to wrap up.

> DINAH

So until next week—

> CARL
>
> [*Still standing and grinning*]

Dinah? . . .

> DINAH

You can sit down, Carl.

> CARL
>
> [*Smile fading*]

You want me to sit down?

> DINAH

Please? I want to say good night to our audience.

> CARL
>
> [*Miffed*]

You mean this is it? You had me drive all the way down here just to take a bow?

> DINAH

What did you expect?

> CARL
>
> [*Peeved*]

I don't know . . . I thought maybe Ralph Edwards was going to pop up . . . and grab me for his show.

> DINAH

Well, he's not here . . .

> CARL

I'm not going be on *This Is Your Life*?

DINAH

Sorry, Carl . . .

Acting angry and disappointed, I stomped off.

For those of you who are too young to remember or don't care to watch TV reruns on hard-to-find cable channels, *This Is Your Life* was one of the most popular and discussed shows of the '50s and '60s. They would surprise a guest, drag him off to a studio where he would watch his past unfold as relatives and friends were paraded out to sing his praises. They were most clever about where and how they would trap their subjects.

The following day, after feigning disappointment about not being chosen as a subject for *This Is Your Life,* my wife called me at work and told me that someone at the *This Is Your Life* office had called.

"Carl, the producers want to make you the subject of one of their upcoming shows and they want my help."

He had entreated her to keep his secret, but my wife reasoned that since she cared more about me than the voice on the phone, she tattled.

It is widely believed that the satire we did of *This Is Your Life,* on *Your Show of Shows,* with Sid Caesar as the reluctant subject and myself parodying the host, Ralph Edwards, was one of the funniest sketches of all time. I knew that if I allowed myself to be a subject on *This Is Your Life,* Sid and all his great writers would sue to revoke my comedy license! I felt strongly about that, or, I should say, I *thought* I felt strongly, before Estelle suggested we discuss it further.

"So honey, what do you think?" she asked timidly.

"What I've always thought. Comedy people are supposed to make fun of these shows, not be on them."

"I couldn't agree more, Carl. But . . . they . . ."

"But they what?"

"Well, they offered to buy you a new car."

"We've got a new car."

"I told them that, but they say—"

"I don't care what *they* say! What *did* they say?"

"That they'd present you with a sixteen-millimeter projector and a film of the event."

"A boring event I'd be embarrassed to be a part of . . . What else?"

When I heard myself ask "What else?" I knew I was weakening and looking to hear better reasons for me to change my mind, which Estelle hastened to furnish.

"Free plane fares and deluxe accommodations at the Hollywood Roosevelt Hotel for your brother and his wife and your friends Lenny Grotte and Joe Coogan. . . ."

I was nine-tenths sold when she said the part about free plane fares and hotel rooms for Charlie and Ilse, and Lenny, my Bronx boyhood chum who had moved to Buffalo and I hadn't seen in years, and Joe Coogan, my dearest army buddy. The clincher came when Estelle added,

"And they asked me if, instead of a car, they could get you something you really would love to have. I told them that you loved Mark Twain, and they called back to say they've found the definitive, complete works of Mark Twain in thirty-six leather-bound volumes, which included his signature and an original manuscript page bound into one of the volumes."

It was difficult living with this secret, this lie! We told no one, not the children, not my parents, not my co-writer, Charley Isaacs, not Dinah, not anyone. I went about my business behaving as if I didn't know that in the next few weeks Ralph Edwards would pop up somewhere, maybe at a fake surprise party for a good friend, and scream at me, "This is your life, Carl Reiner!"

That week, after I had learned about Ralph Edwards's plan, I was on Dinah's show as the "not-so-special guest star." It was a particularly stressful week for me as it always is when I'm required to sing. The song, to be sung as a round, was "No Two People Have Ever Been So in Love." Dinah and I were to be one of three angry couples who make up after escaping from a stuck elevator. The other couples were Gordon and Sheila McCrea and Joey Bishop and Janis Paige. That night, I was concentrating hard on not going off-key, and I didn't. When the song ended we all hugged and kissed while the audience applauded. I was so happy that I didn't screw up that I hugged Dinah extra hard. Instead of letting go I started nuzzling her neck, which made her giggle and the audience laugh. I milked the laugh by nuzzling more fervently as Dinah struggled to read the closing remarks, remarks we had not written!

"Read the cue cards," I whispered while nuzzling away, "some funny lines there."

I was buried in her neck, and all I heard was her ad-libbing something about last week's show and how upset Carl Reiner was about coming to the show just to take a bow. I remember thinking, *Oh, boy, is Charlie Isaacs going to be pissed. He hates it when good jokes are replaced by weak ad-libs.* It was then that I heard a familiar voice announce, "This is Your Life Carl Reiner!" I was not only surprised, I was thunderstruck. I thought, *How in the world could a show that ordinarily requires weeks of preparation be readied in just five days?*

As I was whisked off Stage 4 and ushered down the hall to another stage at the NBC studios, I thought of my parents, who could not be talked into getting on a plane, and wondered what excuse they gave for not being able to come. I also wondered how Ralph Edwards managed to collect enough guests and information about my life to make a worthwhile show. I wondered who they did get? Do I tell Dinah or my friends or relatives that I knew I was going to be on the program because my wife told me? Or do I take the lie to my grave?

I was right about the show, it was rather boring. It seems, to borrow a phrase from Mark Twain, I had, "neglected my bad habits." I had no alcohol or drug addictions and so no rehabilitation stories to tell or any heroic war stories or major diseases that I beat because of my deep faith in the Almighty. I was happy to see my brother and his wife and my friend Lenny and my army buddy Joe Coogan and my old boss, Mr. Weglinsky, and I was not surprised to hear Ralph Edwards say, "Your mom and dad were unable to travel because they are just getting over a flu."

I called them immediately after the show and they were thrilled to see Annie and Robbie looking so pretty and handsome and Estelle so glowing and pregnant, carrying somebody called Lucas, whose birth coincided with the birth of the *Dick Van Dyke Show*, proving again my premise that great children begat great jobs.

All in all, being on *This Is Your Life* was a positive experience. Besides the good memories, I also have a shelfful of books by America's greatest humorist. The producer made a point of telling me how much he paid for them and how they will increase in value. I don't know if he was right, and I am not curious to find out. I love my books—and I love my children who will inherit them.

One last memory. When I called my folks after the show and told them that I didn't expect them to come, knowing how my mother feels about flying, my father surprised me by saying that they would have flown out if they hadn't come down with a terrible flu.

"We both ran very high fevers," he said,

"Pa, c'mon, you really had the flu?" I said, doubting him.

"A bad one. Momma couldn't keep any food down. I had to call our doctor!"

That phrase stopped me cold. Normally, whenever any of us took ill, my father, with help from his best friend, Mr. Glantz, the pharmacist, managed to diagnose and administer all the right medicines without ever calling in a doctor. I knew I had to investigate further.

This following exchange is 90 percent verbatim.

"Pa, who do you mean by 'our doctor'? Mr. Glantz?"

"Not Mr. Glantz, our family doctor."

"We don't have a family doctor!"

"No? And what is Dr. Neushatz?"

"Dr. Neushatz? The doctor who delivered Charlie, and me?"

"That's right, we called him."

"You haven't called Dr. Neushatz in almost forty years,"

"But he's still our family doctor. We'd never call anybody else."

"How did you find him?"

"We looked him up in the phone book."

"He must be a hundred years old."

"He's ninety-six."

"And he still practices?"

"No, he retired ten years ago. He sold his practice and he recommended the doctor who bought it. A lovely young man. He made a house call, gave us a shot of antibiotic, and we're fine now."

———

I don't know why I included the above conversation in this piece. Yes, I do. It's about my father, a very unusual and talented man, and it is a preview of "Perpetual Papa" (Chapter 23), which chronicles his moderately successful attempt to create perpetual motion.

Oh, Mary, Mary, I Am So Sorry

One of the things I am most proud of is my ability to choose wives. I chose a perfect one for myself and an even more perfect one for Dick Van Dyke—of course I mean for Rob Petrie, the character he played on the show that bore his name. I say "more perfect" because my marriage still requires a fair amount of attention and problem solving, whereas the Petries go blithely on and on in a place called TV Land, where all their problems were presolved and nothing is required of them except to go on and on and, hopefully, on and on and on. Before I chose Mary Tyler Moore to play the role of Laura Petrie, I saw forty thousand actresses. I am aware that those we now call actors once were called actresses. For the nonce, I will continue to refer to actors with breasts and stockinged legs as actresses.

I didn't really see forty thousand actresses, it was more like forty. To make myself seem more astute, I exaggerate a bit each time I tell this story. Actually this is not about my brilliant casting of Mary Tyler Moore to play the part of Laura but about the concerns of a writer-producer of a series who is desperate to keep a stage full of talented, sensitive, temperamental and absolutely indispensible artists happy with their decision to sign five-year contracts. The most difficult period for any new show is the first year when the show is thrashing about looking for its soul and its audience. I was most fortunate to have had Sheldon Leonard as my executive producer. Sheldon knew the ropes and knew what to do if the ropes became knotted. Since Sheldon was also the executive producer of a half dozen other shows, he expected that any of the knotty personal and artistic problems that arose would be handled by the writer-producer of each show. By the way, today these writer-producers prefer to call themselves show runners. I believe they do this to differentiate themselves from the producers, co-producers, executive producers, co-executive producers, associate producers, co-associate producers, and the dozens of other assistant and co-assistants and co-co-assistants whose main function is to squeeze as many names as possible into the opening and closing credits.

That first year our show had some problems. For the most part, I was able to solve them without calling in the muscle, Sheldon and our other partner, Danny Thomas. Danny, I should mention, was the one who suggested I see "this girl with the three names, whose legs were featured on the *Richard Diamond Show.*" Mary had been considered to play Danny Thomas's daughter on his show *Make Room for Daddy*, but she lost by a nose. Wrong size and wrong tilt to have been born of Danny's DNA.

Mary was the last of the small army of actresses I saw for the part. After hearing her read the first two lines of the script, I knew we had found our Laura. Mary was the last actress hired for what became a dream cast. The casting of Dick Van Dyke and Rose Marie were Sheldon Leonard's suggestions, Morey Amsterdam was Rose Marie's, and I signed off on all of them, including my suggestion that I play their egocentric boss, Alan Brady.

Very early on I learned one thing about being a producer. When things are going well, you are rarely called upon to meet with a network head or a sponsor or any of the actors. When actors are unhappy about a particular script, they will sometimes ask to have a one-on-one to discuss how shitty their part is and what you are going to do about it. When a show is doing really well, the possibility of an actor asking for a renegotiation of his contract is not uncommon and requires an uncomfortable face-to-face meeting. The meeting you most dread, the one that strikes fear into the black hearts of all producers who have worked hard to mount a successful show, is the meeting that has been requested by one of the show's young stars whose talent and appeal is undeniable. She knows it, because she has read it in all the reviews and featured articles her money-hungry agent cut out and sent her. Unlike myself and Herman Levin, the producer of *Call Me Mister,* I had no oral contract with Mary that forbade her even to think about asking for a raise. I worried that she might ask me, as a dear friend and ally, to release her from her contract so she could accept an offer from a major film studio to play a major role in a major movie. I had never had such a meeting, but one hectic day, while I was doing a rewrite of a scene for the following week's show, my secretary, Peggy Crider, buzzed and told me that Mary Tyler Moore was on the phone and wanted to speak to me. It was the first time that Mary had ever asked to speak with me on the phone, and instinctively I knew it was bad news. I hoped it was about the script, but we always dealt with script problems on the set after a run-through. I wondered what the heck she wanted.

Many things popped into my head as I headed for the phone, among them the smashing photo of Mary on the cover of *Look* magazine and the positive things that were said about her. There was no question in my mind that Mary was destined to have a remarkable career in films or on Broadway. As I picked up the phone, I hoped she wasn't going to tell me that she wanted to start her remarkable career in films this week.

"Hey, Mary," I said, cheerily, "what's up?"

"I can't tell you on the phone," she said somberly, "may I come to your office?"

"Of course. Is something wrong?"

"Well," she hesitated, "yes, there is, but I'd rather not discuss this on the phone."

"I understand, please come up."

While waiting for Mary to make the trek from Stage 8 of the Desilu Cahuenga Studios to my office on the second floor of a building that was less than a hundred yards away, I girded myself to deal with the worst-case scenario. I decided that I would listen patiently and sympathetically to whatever she had to say, but I would not shirk my responsibility to the show; the other cast members; my partners, Dick, Sheldon, and Danny; and most importantly, to myself. Though I was very fond of Mary, I had worked too hard helping make this show a success to compromise it by being a good guy and letting Mary go, even if it was to fly "somewhere over the rainbow."

During working hours, we found that 61 percent of the time, Mary had this wonderful, broad smile on her face. As she settled into a club chair in my office, her smile that we know from the main title of her own show could "light the world up," was now a sickly one that could barely light up a corner of my office.

"So, Mary, what did you want to see me about?" I asked.

"I wanted to tell you something that I thought you should know," she replied, looking first at me, then at her hands. "Only a few people know about my decision, and I wanted you to know before the press get hold of it . . ."

On our show, I had written many lines of dialogue for Mary's character and now in my head I was continuing to write her dialogue: *"Carl, my agent wanted to speak to you about this, but I thought that since we have this relationship, it would be better coming from me. I . . . I don't know how to say this—it may not be fair—but I have been offered the lead in a big MGM musical opposite Gene Kelly, and I would like to . . ."*

I was sure that some upsetting news of this nature was coming, but I wasn't sure of how I'd handle it.

"This had been coming on even before I started the show," Mary said, looking directly at me, "and I didn't tell anybody about it, because I thought we might be able to work it out . . . but . . . I couldn't. . . . Carl, I am leaving Richard . . . Richard and I . . ."

In the split second before she continued, I panicked and thought she was talking about Dick Van Dyke, referring to him as Richard because she was angry with him for some reason. My five-second reverie was interrupted by Mary's voice saying, ". . . have decided to divorce."

There were tears in Mary's eyes. I mirrored her emotions, but the tears in my eyes were tears of joy at discovering she was talking about her husband, Richard, and not my Richard. My voice had a proper tone of sadness in it when I said, "Oh, Mary, I am so sorry." Fair actor that I am, I was able to hide the selfish-bastard side of myself while showing concern for her immediate needs and assuring her of our continued friendship and support. Mary, dear heart, was worried that the publicity might hurt the show.

I never discussed with Mary my dual reaction to her telling me that upsetting piece of news until now.

July 14, 2002

Dear, dear Mary,

For allowing myself to feel unmitigated joy that day forty-one years ago when you were feeling unimaginable pain, I humbly offer you my extremely belated but most sincere apology.

     Love,

     Carl

P.S. Mary, I was thinking I'd end this with "Well, that's show biz!" What do you think?

12

My Son, the Hall of Famer

I was seated at my desk doing writer-producer things for an upcoming episode of *The Dick Van Dyke Show* when I received a phone call from someone in New York informing me that I had been chosen to receive the first Hall of Fame Award from my alma mater, Evander Childs High School. The pleasant voice on the phone told me that the other candidates for the award were a state Supreme Court justice, a former Miss America, and a beloved actor-comedian, whose real name was Aaron Chwatt. I don't remember the name of the judge but the Miss America was Bess Meyerson, and Aaron Chwatt was Red Buttons. I was flattered, of course, but I wondered, *Why did they choose me?* Immediately, I heard my mother's voice answer, "Because you're the best one!"

My mother always felt that I was underappreciated. After watching *Your Show of Shows*, Mom never missed an opportunity to offer me advice and compliments. Our conversations were frequent and repetitious.

"Carl, they didn't give you enough to do this week."

"Ma, I had a lot to do this week. Did you like the show?"

"It was a good show, but it would be a better show if they put you in more skits."

"They're called sketches, Ma, and I was in three of them this week."

"With small parts, they should give you bigger parts! Tell them that everybody I talk to raves about how good you are . . . and smart. The other day," she said, proudly, "a lady I met in Crotona Park asked me, where you learned to speak all those languages, Italian and French and German?"

"Ma, did you tell her that I can't speak those languages and that I was doing double-talk?"

"Why does she have to know?"

"Because lots of people speak French and Italian and German, Ma. Very few people can do double-talk."

"Let her think what she wants. Who does it hurt?"

It's clear that Mom preferred that people think of her son as smart and educated rather than funny.

My mother was illiterate and was able, somehow, to keep that secret from most people, including my brother and me. It wasn't until Charlie and I were teenagers that we compared notes and agreed, "Hey, Mom can't read!" Whenever there was something either of us wanted Mom to read, she would say, "Read it to me, I don't have my glasses," or "I'm busy ironing, you read, I'll listen," or "Leave it on the couch, I'll read it later."

For some reason, perhaps because we sensed that Mom felt ashamed, Charlie and I never discussed her illiteracy with either her or my father.

Mom was one of nine siblings, four brothers and five sisters, and because she was the prettiest of the girls and had an upturned nose, was dubbed the Princess. The Princess was born in Bucharest, Romania, where, as a young child, she had the first of two dramatic and, I am certain, personality-shaping experiences. She remembered clearly her mother putting her inside a cold oven when she was three years old and telling her that she must not talk or make a sound. Many a Jewish household lived in fear of Cossack-like marauders riding into town to make trouble. Rampant were the stories of hoodlums grabbing infants from their cribs and smashing their heads against a tree trunk or a wall. It was not uncommon for terrified parents to hide their precious infants in places like potato bins, attics, closets, and stoves.

The Princess emigrated with her family to America in 1901 and completed her formal education at the age of seven. At eight, after receiving a diploma from her first grade class, which Mom had framed and I now own, she secured a job as a finisher in a factory that manufactured American flags. A finisher was an unskilled worker who finished what the skilled worker, the seamstress, was not required to do, snip off all the loose threads that hung from the new Grand Old Flags. Because of the child labor laws, enforcers from the Geary Society would sweep through sweatshops looking for exploited children. The exploiting factory owners were always tipped off when a visit was imminent, and they prepared for the inspection by hiding their child laborers. Bessie Mathias, the Princess, was trained to climb into a giant canvas bin, lie prone on the bottom, and remain quiet and motionless under the hundreds of finished, unfolded flags that would be dumped on top of her. Having to struggle for air while struggling to earn a few cents a day, I imagine, does not engender any sense of security in an eight-year-old.

My mother lived her life fearing the worst. She was certain

that disaster was lurking for my brother and me everywhere, at every street crossing, in every schoolyard, in every strange neighborhood, and even in our own neighborhood after dark.

A sad, touching clue to my mom's illiteracy presented itself after she received a copy of my novel *Enter Laughing*, a fictionalized version of my young life. I was concerned how my parents might react to the way I depicted some of the fictional family members.

"The book was wonderful!" Mom phoned to say. "Congratulations!"

"Oh, thanks, Mom, you've read it?"

"Of course we read it," she said defensively, "why wouldn't we read it?"

"Well, I just gave it to you a couple of days ago . . ."

"And we finished it today—Papa read it out loud—half yesterday and half today. It's very good—a very nice story."

"You really liked it?"

"Who wouldn't like it?" Mom challenged, "It's a very nice story—true to life—but the book . . ."

"What about the book, Ma?"

"Well, I think you made a mistake and sent us Estelle's book. She probably has ours."

"Estelle's book? Ma, I don't understand."

"In the book we have, it says 'To Estelle.' You must have mixed them up."

Never having read a book, Mom did not know that "To Estelle," which my father had read aloud, was the printed dedication and not, as she imagined, one I wrote by hand.

I have not yet thought about to whom I will dedicate this book, but I know Bessie Reiner's name will be first.

———

The day I was needed to attend the Evander Childs Hall of Fame ceremony in the Bronx conflicted with my responsibilities to the *Dick Van Dyke Show* in Los Angeles. Reluctantly, I had to decline the honor, and was touched when the disappointed Hall of Fame chairperson assured me that I would be installed as their first honoree, whether or not I appeared in person.

And because fate stepped in, in the guise of CBS's publicity department, I was able to appear in person. Ordinarily, we shot six episodes in a row and took a week off, but to accommodate the publicity department, they arranged for us to take a few extra days and fly to New York to do interviews and television appearances. I immediately called the Hall of Fame people and informed them that I would be attending the ceremony.

While still in Los Angeles, I jotted down the day and the time I was due to be at my high school—Wednesday at 11:00 A.M. In the two days bracketing the Hall of Fame event I had quite a few appointments and interviews, all neatly typed in an itinerary CBS had prepared. We arrived in New York rather late and checked into my favorite Manhattan hotel, the Algonquin, home of the legendary Round Table. I saw the legendary table but none of the legends.

I awoke early the next morning and called the car service to say that since it looked like it might rain, we should leave no later than 9:30.

The dispatcher started to question my decision, and I politely insisted that I had to get to Evander Childs High School on Gun Hill Road in the Bronx no later than 10:45 and to send the car now!

While I showered, shaved, gobbled a quick breakfast, dressed myself in a white shirt, blue suit, and a regimental tie,

I thought about the students who would be attending the ceremony, and what I might say to them.

I asked myself, *Do I have any inspirational words of wit and wisdom that these teenagers might find amusing and would also have some substance—serious thoughts that might be of some help in planning their future?*

The answer came back to me loudly and clearly.

No! You can't do that! You'll do what you always do, bullshit! Just hope it's the kind that has some fertilizing nutrients in it.

On the ride from Manhattan to my old Bronx high school, I thought about how much the limo ride was costing and how different my life had been when I was young. From 1936 until I graduated in June of 1938, for one nickel I rode to school each morning on the Third Avenue El (elevated train) from Tremont Avenue to Gun Hill Road. In my junior and senior years, during the spring and autumn months, I saved a nickel a day by walking home from school, which took under an hour. A nickel doesn't sound like much, but by the end of the month, you've got a pretty tidy sum. In the midst of a major depression, a dollar can get you into a couple of movies, buy a bag of White Castle hamburgers, some candy bars, sodas, and if you had a girl who liked you, a dutch-treat date.

We arrived at the front entrance of the school, and I expected that it would look a lot smaller than I remembered it, but it didn't. It looked exactly as impressive and forbidding. There were about twenty steps in the wide stairway that led to the four sets of entrance doors. I had not called ahead to say exactly what time I would arrive, so did not expect a welcoming committee, but I did expect to see a few students milling about. I was about twenty minutes early, and I assumed that everyone was either on their way to the assembly hall or filing into it.

Since I was told that the ceremony would not be a long one, I suggested that the limo driver stay right where he was. I bounded up the stairs, and was strangely moved by this simple act of going into a building I had not been in for twenty-five years. The assembly hall was where it always was: directly across from the front entrance. The assembly hall doors had little windows in them, and before dashing in, I looked in to see how many students had assembled, and all I could see were portraits of Washington and Lincoln looking back at me. Not one student had assembled!

"Where the heck is everybody?" I mumbled to no one as I looked at my watch and wondered why the assembly hall was empty and dark.

It was twenty minutes to eleven! Unless, *unless* I hadn't reset my watch correctly. Before landing, I had reset my watch for New York time, three hours forward—or—did I set it forward only two hours, making the time now not ten minutes to eleven, but ten minutes to *ten*?! That it! It's *ten of ten!*—*No! It's not!* The limo driver didn't fly across the country and reset his watch. I told him to be at the hotel at 9:30 A.M. and that's when he came and it took an hour to get here!

I checked my watch again, and saw that it was twenty minutes to eleven . . . and I also saw that it was Tuesday.

Tuesday! the voice inside my head, shouted, *Today is Tuesday, not Wednesday, you fool!*

That is why the dispatcher was hesitant about sending the limo this morning. He had the reservation for Wednesday. I was so concerned about being late, and I ended up being one day and twenty minutes too early! I felt like an idiot.

All I could think of was how I might leave the scene of my stupidity without being seen. I wanted desperately to undo the whole experience. I'm sure you won't believe how I attempted to accomplish this, but what I did was, and I'm not making this up, try to visualize myself on film and reversing the film. I laughed to myself as I backed away from the auditorium and continued to walk backward across the hallway, out the front doors, down the entire flight of stairs, and toward the limo. The confused but bemused chauffeur had watched the proceedings and accommodated my madness by holding the door open while I backed in.

After he concurred that it was Tuesday, I shouted "Let's go!" and we drove off.

"If, by chance, someone saw me walking backward, I would, naturally, be embarrassed, but," I explained to the chauffeur, so he wouldn't think me a complete nut, "instead of running off, I would stop and tell him, why I was doing what I was doing and, perhaps get a chuckle or two out of him. I got one from you, didn't I?"

"You did." He smiled.

"I think that inviting people to laugh *with* you while you're laughing *at* yourself is a good thing to do. You're still the fool, but you're the fool in charge."

The following morning, wearing the same clothes and being driven by the same chauffeur, I was armed with a premise for my little speech. This time, I was royally greeted on the front steps by a gracious welcoming committee, who ushered me into the auditorium. After a couple of announcements, I was given an embarrassingly complimentary introduction by the school principal, who invited me to come to the podium to accept the award. He informed the students that, "Mr. Reiner, I'm sure, has some remarks he would like to make."

My 'remarks' started by my telling the students how thrilled I was to be chosen for Evander Childs's first Hall of Fame Award.

"You know," I said, smiling broadly, "I was so excited about coming back to my old school that I could not wait for today—and I didn't! I came yesterday! I thought yesterday was today but, as you all know, today is today. I wasn't off by much."

While telling of my premature visit to their school, I did an impression of myself alighting from the limousine and jauntily bounding up the front steps, and confidently striding to the assembly hall, and, on seeing it empty and discovering that it was Tuesday, I confidently backed away from the hall. They laughed as I strutted backward around the stage to illustrate how I must have looked going out of the building backward, and continuing in this mode, down the steps, "and into the limo for a quick getaway before any of you guys saw me."

By admitting that I was a goofy kind of kid who still did goofy things, I offered myself as living proof that one can make it in life,

    even if you did not get high enough grades to be accepted by CCNY, a tuition-free city college;

    even if you never went out for a team or joined the Chess Club or became involved in any of the extracurricular school activities;

    even if you did not apply to audition for the Drama Club, because you were sure you would be rejected;

    even if you squeaked through your junior high school algebra class without ever finding out what X stood for;

    even if you end a sentence with a preposition, as I did in the last even-if;

    even if you once competed against thirteen others in an amateur contest and came in thirteenth;

    even if you had a crush on a girl, (Selma Futerman) for

the whole time you were in school and never once spoke to her, because you thought you might not be her type.

I am not sure the principal and the teachers appreciated my lighthearted acceptance of a premise that not everything that we perceive as failure is that, but the kids were sure enjoying an uninspirational talk by a Hall of Famer, who, in essence, was telling them that by just being themselves, they could make it.

I never did any kind of survey or follow-up on those students, so I will never know how much harm I did them . . . or good?

13

Three Macho Cowards

The Place: San Francisco airport
The Time: Sunday, 11:00 P.M., summer of 1965

Eva Marie Saint, Brian Keith, Norman Jewison, and I had just arrived from Los Angeles, having spent the weekend with our families. We were on our way back to northern California where, for the past few weeks, we had been on location filming *The Russians Are Coming, the Russians Are Coming!* On preparing to board the small plane for the connecting flight to Fort Bragg, a trip we had made without incident several times during the twelve-week shooting schedule, we were informed that there was going to be a "change of equipment." It was unsettling to hear about problems with the "equipment"—and who decided to call a big thing like an airplane "equipment"?

Ordinarily, the "equipment" we flew on was a twin-engine Beechcraft, but it seemed that the Beechcraft and our regular pilot were both ailing and unavailable. We were assured that the replacement pilot and plane, a single-engine Cessna, were quite capable of getting us safely to the Wilmot Airport in Eureka. The small plane could uncomfortably accommodate four passengers. The least uncomfortable seat was the one next to the pilot. We, being gallant "guys," insisted that the "doll," Eva Marie Saint, sit in the cockpit. Brian Keith and I sat on a benchlike middle seat, and Norman Jewison, the narrowest of us, volunteered to sit behind us on the little fold-down jump seat, under which I stowed a shoe box containing a present I had bought for my six-year-old son, Lucas—a pair of cowboy boots that needed to be exchanged for the right size and the right color.

From a nervous passenger's point of view, it was a rotten night for flying, but our pilot did not seem at all concerned that it was drizzling and the wind socks on the landing strip were plump and flapping in the breeze and that a fog appeared to be rolling in. We macho guys all made jaunty comments about enjoying the adventure of taking off and flying in bad weather, and I wondered if I was the only one who was lying. Probably. Brian Keith, a very fine actor, an excellent drinker, and a rock steady man's man, seemed to be his cool, confident self—as was Norman Jewison, a happy-go-lucky Canadian, inured to pain and freezing winters—and Eva Marie Saint, whose composure and strength are built into her name. All seemed totally at ease, which had a calming effect on me.

I was not happy to hear that the flying time in our single-engine Cessna would be a bit longer than with the Beechcraft. In spite of the wind and rain, we were cleared for takeoff and our pilot—whose name I didn't hear though it sounded like Poncho or Ponchus, so I thought of him as Pontius pilot—Pontius pushed the throttle forward, and we started down the bumpy runway. As the plane picked up speed, the windshield was splattered with giant raindrops. What was a light drizzle had suddenly turned into a heavy downpour. The single-engine plane shuddered as it took off and immediately started swaying drunkenly from side to side, bouncing and bumping as it struggled to climb higher. The cabin became eerily silent. The pilot was concentrating hard on steadying the vibrating plane, and none of us dared distract him with questions. *"If it keeps bouncing like this, might the wings fall off?"* is one I wanted to ask but held my tongue as did my fellow passengers. After what seemed like hours but was in reality about ten minutes, I found it necessary to break the silence.

"Uh, sir," I asked, mustering a matter-of-fact tone, "what was that string of red lights we just passed—at eye level? I don't remember seeing those red lights on any of our previous flights."

"Oh, they were there," the pilot assured me, "but you were probably flying a couple of thousand feet above them."

"What are they?" all of us asked.

"Santa Rosa airport's warning lights," Pontius advised us calmly, "keeps low-flying planes from crashing into structures lower than five hundred feet."

"Why aren't we up a couple of thousand feet?" I asked.

"Been trying to, but the winds and rain are sort of holding us down," he said. "Might have to stay at this altitude all the way to Eureka. You do have to get there tonight, don't you?"

Brian, Norman, and I agreed that we did. I did so with less enthusiasm.

"If you're nervous about the bumps and bounces," he said, "I could put her down."

Again, each of the macho men, not wanting to appear like spineless wimps, agreed that we push on.

"Hey, fellers, this is a little too bumpy-bouncy for me," Eva said calmly but firmly, "why don't we just land in Santa Rosa and rent a car?"

Without a moment's hesitation, we all spoke up. "Fine

with me, Eva." "If that's what you want." "If you're uncomfortable . . ."

On hearing our response, the pilot banked the plane sharply, made a U-turn and nosed the "equipment" toward the Santa Rosa airport. None of us were prepared for that kamikaze maneuver, and we found ourselves suddenly lying on our right sides. Accompanying the passenger's grunts and groans were the frightening sounds of a door flying open, a sudden rush of air, and a whooshing noise. It sounded as though something slid along the floor and bumped against the flapping door. The most disturbing sound of all was the "*Oh shit!*" that escaped from Norman Jewison a split second after hearing the sliding-whooshing sound. All this activity happened directly behind my seat. Trying to be heard above the sound of the motor and the rushing air, I screamed, "*Norman are you all right?*" Getting no response, I twisted my head and body around as far as my seat belt would allow and saw—no Norman! I heard the sound of the small cargo door flapping against the fuselage as I reached behind me and swung my arm back and forth, trying to touch Norman, all the while, screaming, "*Norman, are you there? Say something!*"

I will not vouch for the accuracy of all the dialogue in this scene, but I do remember announcing these words to my terrified friends: "*I think we lost Norman!*" I had good reason to believe that Norman had slid out of the plane, because all of the evidence supported this—The sliding, whooshing sound, the open cargo door flapping against the fuselage, and his not answering when I screamed his name. I continued to call his name as I loosened my belt and got into a position to see what the hell had happened—and what I saw sent a chill through me. Norman was not in his jump seat—the seat had sprung back up. My fear that Norman had fallen out of the plane was half-justified. Half of Norman was hanging outside the plane facedown and his bottom half was stretched out on the floor. His right hand was reaching for and vainly grabbing at the handle of the swinging cargo door. I held onto his belt as he continued being assaulted by a driving rain, a gale force wind, and the wash from the propeller. The elements were doing all they could to frustrate him but our dogged, rain-soaked director, leaning out dangerously far, finally managed to catch the door handle. With minimum help from me, he shimmied his way back into the plane and pulled the door shut. He grimaced, and said, "Lost your kid's boots, sorry."

When the pilot had made his unannounced, fighter-pilot maneuver, the rubber bands that had been securing the cargo door snapped, the door flew open, and the sliding-whooshing sound I thought was Norman going to his death was made by the box of boots sliding along the floor and out the door.

I told Norman Jewison then, and I have told him many times since, that I would rather have lost fifty pair of boots than have lost the indispensable services of the director of *The Russians Are Coming, the Russians Are Coming*—the one and only movie on which I was given what appeared to be top billing.

14

The Deadly Friendly Game

After living through Norman Jewison's out-of-plane, out-of-body experience, we all endured another eight hours of terror being chauffeured to Fort Bragg by Brian Keith, one of the Macho Men, who never figured out which knobs controlled the radio, the air-conditioner, the horn, or the defogger. He steered the rented Buick in a heavy downpour, through cotton-candy fog, over tortuous mountain roads. To avoid veering off a cliff, he drove at six miles an hour while straddling the white line in the center of the two-lane road. I stared intently at that white line for most of the trip and when we finally arrived at our motel, I felt like a hypnotized chicken. All of us were tired, grungy, and bedraggled. We had arrived on time and ready to shoot—but the company wasn't. The insistent rain had made it impossible to shoot the scheduled exterior scenes that day or the next or the next. We had risked our lives for nothing!

Recalling the day of our traumatic plane and car rides and our arrival at Fort Bragg, triggered a memory of an extraordinary gathering that took place in my motel suite on a dark, rainy afternoon.

Present in the cramped living room of my motel suite were many of the film's actors, among them, Jonathan Winters, Alan Arkin, Theodore Bickel, Michael J. Pollard, Paul Ford, Cliff Norton, Richard Schall, and three of the Cessna Four, Eva Marie Saint, Brian Keith and myself. Norman Jewison was off somewhere cursing and worrying, the only thing a director can do when horrible weather screws up his shooting schedule.

Hearing complaints about how little there is to do on rainy days in a small, quaint town whose one movie theater is only open at night, I thought it would be nice to invite the bored cast members to my room to discuss antidotes to boredom, nibble Chee-tos and whatever else room service could provide, and perhaps, play a game or two. When someone said, "How about we play charades?" someone countered with "How about fuck charades?" and everyone agreed it was a lousy idea, including me, who suggested it.

I don't know what possessed me to suggest another game, but I did.

"Hey," I announced, "I know a game we can play that I bet you haven't played for a long time. I think it's the kind of a game that, if we play seriously, could be very exciting and something we'll all remember fondly."

Here now is how I introduced the playing of ring around the rosy to the cast of *The Russians Are Coming, the Russians Are Coming.*

"All right, gang," I said, "raise your hands if you don't know how to play ring around the rosy."

Some raised their hands, some raised their eyebrows, some laughed, and some did all three.

"When was the last time any of you played a really serious game of ring around the rosy?" was my next question.

All admitted that they had not played it since they were children, and some recalled playing it with their own children.

"But you have never played it with adults," I pointed out, "and I guarantee that if you do, you will find it a hundred times more satisfying than it ever was. So do I have any players for a serious game of ring around the rosy?"

And what a gemütlich group they were! I believe Eva Marie Saint and Theodore Bikel were the first to volunteer and were closely followed by Alan Arkin, Cliff Norton, Jonathan Winters, et al. To make room for our game, I moved all the chairs and tables aside and without being instructed all the players joined hands and formed an almost perfect circle. I believe one or two of them laughed. I was upset by their attitude, but I chose not to admonish them at this time. I stepped between two of those gigglers, took their hands and joined the group.

"Now, does anyone not know the lyrics to the song?" Jonathan Winters said he was sure he remembered them all but had a question.

"After 'Ashes, ashes,' some little kids sang 'aw faw dow' instead of 'all fall down.' Which is preferred?"

"Either is acceptable, but I think the latter, 'all fall down' suits our group better. Okay, gang," I said, masking my excitement, "we'll do a practice round, at half speed, and we will circle to the right!"

"It's not going to be easy to fall down at half speed," Alan Arkin advised. "Should we just indicate falling down?"

"Right, Alan," I agreed, "we won't fall on this rehearsal. Ready? Ring around the . . ."

We had barely sung the first line when someone, I think it was Alan Arkin, started to laugh.

"Hold it, hold it!" I said, controlling my anger "I didn't think I had to spell it out, but for this game to be fun, we have to play it seriously. If you don't think you can be serious, then you can all leave and we'll forget about it. Is that what you want? I think you'll be missing out on something special. What'll it be?"

Reluctantly, they all agreed to give it a go.

"Very well, we are understood," I said, hopefully, "let's try again. Ring . . . around . . . the . . . rohh-sy . . . a pocket full of pohhsy . . ."

The group went through the mock rehearsal and waited for my critique.

"Well, well," I started, feigning disappointment, "that first attempt at playing the game was shoddy, which is what I anticipated but what I find unforgivable is the fact that half of the actors, who think of themselves as disciplined profession-als, either suppressed giggles or laughed openly—and this, after I warned you of the consequences. I guess playing a seri-ous game of ring around the rosy with you people is just not possible. Why don't you all go back to your suites and bore yourselves to sleep."

I started to open the motel door but turned back to deliver my parting thrust, which I delivered sincerely and with pas-sion. "In case some of you've forgotten the origin of this song, let me refresh your memory. In the fifteenth century, the bubonic plague decimated half the population in the world and this charming little ditty, which was sung and performed by innocent English schoolchildren, described what hap-pened to a victim after being infected with the plague. Little red spots would appear on the skin—ring around the rosy— followed by death and flowers—pocket full of posies—and finally, the cremation of the ashen-faced corpse—ashes, ashes, all fall down! I guess"—I sighed resignedly—"you have all forgotten why it should be sung and played seriously but if you can't be serious . . ."

"We can, we can!" "We'll be serious!" "Give us another chance!"

I will never forget being a part of this group of dedicated, mature actors circling about as we sang a sober and dignified rendition of ring around the rosy. We sang it not once but four times, circling first to the right and then to the left and each time falling down. The final rendition was the most difficult because by that time none of us could hold back the laughter that started building when we first agreed to be serious about acting silly.

15

Type Me a Broadway Play

There is an open wound in my psyche, a critic-inflicted or perhaps self-inflicted wound that has defied the healing laws of nature and time. By having the last printed word on the subject, I am confident that the old wound will close, and I will live happily ever after. We'll see.

If you were attending theater in New Haven, Boston or New York in 1967, there is a possibility that you might have seen *Something Different*, the one and only play I ever wrote for the legitimate theater. Of all the experiences I've had in show business, the writing and directing of *Something Different* was by far the most memorable. In terms of excitement, terror, joy, sadness, anger, frustration, elation, and depression, nothing even comes close. I daresay that no Broadway play has ever had a more bizarre conception. It was a play born not out of any deep desire to write but out of sheer boredom, and not even mine. It was my secretary's, a young lady named Linda Duugles (yes, two *u*'s), who had worked for me during the last year of the *Dick Van Dyke Show* and then in preproduction for *The Comic*. The film was slated to start as soon as our star, Dick Van Dyke, became available, which was estimated to be in two months. Aaron Ruben, my co-writer and co-producer, went back to his executive producer's office for *The Andy Griffith Show*, leaving me to mind the store.

When Aaron and I were writing and rewriting the screenplay, Linda was happily typing and retyping right along with us. It was about three weeks after we had handed in our final draft that Linda said the magic words that started my odyssey.

"Do you have anything for me to type?"

"Not right now." I said.

"Maybe you can find something," she sighed, "I'm so bored."

She said it so wistfully that, to accommodate her need to type, I sat down at my typewriter and started clacking away. (In days or yore, typewriters not only clacked but rang bells). In took me no more than a couple of minutes to mock up something that looked like the beginning of a play. Thoughtfully, I left a fair amount of x'ed-out sentences and typpiographicialll errors for her to correct and retype.

I pulled the page out of my typewriter and dropped it on Linda's desk.

"Stop what you're doing," I barked, "I need two clean copies! *Now!*"

I hurried back to my desk, and while rolling a blank page into my Smith-Corona, I head Linda typing and giggling.

"This is so funny," she said, returning the retyped page, "what is this?"

"A play! You said you wanted something to type, didn't you?"

"Yes," she said, laughing, "but I didn't expect to type a play."

That is precisely how it started, as a joke. I was going to type up a few more pages and give Linda what, in grade school, we called busywork, but later that morning, after hearing Linda laugh as she typed three more pages of my fake play, I realized that I was also onto something; exactly what, I wasn't sure, but I did know it was something different. I was curious to find out where it would go. After Linda left for the day, I stayed on to complete Scene One of *Something Different*. After reading it over I realized that I was writing an absurdist comedy, parodying the absurd dramas that were filling theaters on both sides of the Atlantic. I had seen productions of Becket's *Waiting for Godot*, Ionesco's, *The Rhinoceros*, Duerren-matt's *The Visit*, Pinter's *The Birthday Party*, and Albee's *Tiny Alice* and had been alternately impressed, amused, entertained, and, at times, utterly confused.

By putting in full days of writing and retyping, we managed to complete a three-act play in less than six weeks. My wise agent, Mike Zimring, thought it good enough to send to Alex Cohen, an esteemed Broadway producer, who two nights later phoned me at home and said to me what no writer expects to hear except from a friend who is playing a cruel joke.

"In twenty-five years of reading and producing plays, I have never read a funnier comedy—and neither has my wife, Hildy. I'd like to get it on in September. Are you available to direct it in September?"

Wow! This genius of a producer who, at the age of twenty-one, mounted his first hit, Edward Chodorov's *Kind Lady*, had asked *me* to come to New York to direct *my* play. It was just too good to be true! And it was. . . .

Three weeks after I had told everybody who meant anything to me that I was going to New York to direct my play, I received another call from Alex Cohen who informed me that because of some financial setback, he would be unable to mount our show for a September start but we could in February, if I were available. . . .

A few days after I stopped saying "Shit!" and convincing my loved ones that I really wasn't disappointed because I had known it was too good to be true, my dogged agent Mike Zimring called to tell me that Alan King, Walter Hyman, Gene Wolsk, and Emanuel Azenberg, who had just formed a production company, had read the play, loved it, and if I agreed, "could be ready to start production yesterday!"

On November 28, 1967, *Something Different,* the play I wrote as busywork for my bored secretary, opened at the Cort Theater in New York City. It sported a stellar cast that included Bob Dishy, Linda Lavin, Gabe Dell, Maureen Arthur, Claudia McNeil, Helena Carroll, Victoria Zussin, and Messers Jones, Mansfield, Starkman and Battle, four sets of ten-year-old identical twins. To give you some sense of the play I will, with the permission of Samuel French, Inc., offer a short exchange of dialogue from Act One, Scene Two.

Bud Nemerov (played by Bob Dishy) is a renowned and celebrated playwright—who had written only one play in his life, *Seven Times Seven, Plus One*, which everyone in the world has either seen or read.

In the following scene, Bud, the egocentric and distracted husband and father and his scheming, cuckolding wife, Beth (Linda Lavin), are having an ongoing argument about whether or not their ten-year-old sons are really twins. Bud is suspicious they're not, because one boy is white and redheaded and the other boy is black. Bud is questioning the "twins" as they stand before him.

BUD

Just a moment, children.

KEVIN AND BEVIN

What is it, Dad?

BUD

Why is it you always talk together?

BETH

[*interrupts*]

You know very well, dear, it's because they're twins. Isn't that so, children?

KEVIN AND BEVIN

We're not sure.

BUD

Aha! You're not sure, eh? When's your birthday?

KEVIN AND BEVIN

July 14, 1956.

BUD

How tall are you?

KEVIN AND BEVAN

Ten foot two.

BUD

Ten foot two?

KEVIN AND BEVIN

Together.

BUD

What was the name of the play I wrote before you were born?

KEVIN AND BEVIN

Seven Times Seven.

BUD

Hmmm?

KEVIN AND BEVIN

Plus one.

BUD

How long did it run?

KEVIN AND BEVIN

Four years, nine months, three days.

BUD

How many good reviews did I get?

KEVIN AND BEVIN

Twelve out of twelve.

BUD

Close your eyes. What color is your hair?

KEVIN AND BEVIN

Black and red.

BUD

What color are your legs?

KEVIN AND BEVIN

Black and blue.

BUD

[*Checks legs, finds bruises*]

The scene continues with Bud becoming more and more aware that something is not right in his household.

Early in the first act we learn that for twelve years Bud has tried and failed to write another play. In desperation, he tries to recapture his muse by re-creating the physical conditions he had when he wrote his great play. At that time, he was living in his mother's cramped Bronx apartment, so in an attempt to re-create that atmosphere, he brings into his elegant Scarsdale mansion, among other items, his mother's old coil refrigerator, her kitchen table where he sat when typing his play, a beautiful, buxom actress (Maureen Arthur), whom he hires to play his mother (his actual mother is unavailable to play herself because she lives in Florida), and a dozen cockroaches, which he buys from an exterminator (Gabe Dell).

At our first out-of-town tryout in New Haven, we previewed a three-act play. The first two acts were a satire of plays of the theater of the absurd, and the third act, which I felt was the play's raison d'être, and for me the most innovative part of the package. *Something Different* was a play-within-a-play-within-a-play-within-a-play-within-a-play and I was proud to have written something original. The reaction of the opening-night audience in New Haven was mixed. There were huge laughs in the first two acts and in the third act there were fewer laughs and huge walkouts. Half the audience left and the other half remained to cheer. The cheering half were mainly Yale students who tossed around words like "daring," "imaginative" and "genius," and the other half were older folk tossing around words like "He should be arrested," "Why did you bring me here!" and "Feh!"

In the third act, the exterminator who was playing a Nazi in the play-within-the-play, was beaten to death by the rest of the cast which, to the audience, looked as if it was scripted. However when the curtain came down, a call for a doctor was heard over a loudspeaker and a hush fell over the entire theater as a doctor came on stage and pronounced the actor (Gabe Dell) dead. In the-show-must-go-on tradition, the cast took a curtain call—all but Gabe Dell. A solemn cast, appearing to be genuinely shaken, did not acknowledge the scattered applause but looked toward the wings to where Gabe had been carried. The siren of an approaching ambulance is heard—becoming louder and louder as the final curtain falls.

By the time the show arrived in New Haven, the cast had been rehearsing for four weeks. I had been directing during the day, rewriting during the night and rehearsing new third acts the following day. I averaged three or four hours of sleep a night, and I was ready for someone to tell me how to make "that damn third act work!" I had already written four or five versions, so when two wise old Joes, Stein and Mankiewiecz, came backstage to talk to me after a performance, I listened.

Joe Stein, who had adapted my first novel, *Enter Laughing*, for the stage and Sholem Aleichem's Tevya, (*Fiddler on the Roof*) got to me first.

"Carl, you've got a perfect two-act, Feydeau-type farce," Joe S. advised, "you don't need that third act."

I had never read Feydeau but I assumed he did good work. Joe M., who I didn't know but admired for writing and directing *All about Eve*, told me that I "was digging in sand!"

"No playwright," he informed me, "including Aeschylus, has ever been able to write a satire about a satire. Drop the third act, and you got a hit."

They saved my life, those good Joes.

For the Boston engagement, I took what was good and funny from the third act and mulched the material into the first two acts—and damned if it didn't work! We had a sold-out, laugh-filled two-week run in Boston. Elliot Norton, the venerable drama critic of the *Boston Globe*, did not know what to make of it, and his review reflected his confusion. He called me "a nut cake" and used phrases like, "unparalleled uproar" and "idiotically funny." For some reason, I was not upset and accepted Mr. Norton's gracious invitation to appear with him on his local television show to discuss and/or defend my play. It was positive experience and helped sell tickets.

The show got an unequivocal rave from Frank Rich. Yes, *the* Frank Rich, the powerful and insightful drama critic of *The New York Times*, who terrified playwrights and producers for years and is now an even more brilliant editorialist for the same paper. At that time, Frank Rich was the drama critic of the *Harvard Crimson* and was the first freshman in the history of the school to hold that position. As I say, his review was a rave, and his analysis of the play was superb. I remember thinking *This boy will go far.* Some small-minded people might think that he praised the show so highly because, at that time, he was dating my equally brilliant daughter, Annie, and might have envisioned becoming my son-in-law. Well, sir, Annie, who didn't have to sidle up to me so I would continue to be her father, had the same positive reaction to my play that Frank did.

I would have to say that the Boston critics treated us fairly and helped make our run in their fair city a successful one. However, a different set of critics and a different fate awaited us in New York.

We had many good reasons to feel optimistic about our New York opening. The Boston audiences were going away from our show "good-mouthing" us, and there were other indications that we had a better than fair chance at success. Two of my dear show-business friends, Mel Brooks and Neil Simon, whose opinions I valued, did not seem to be lying when they told me that they loved the show. I do know for certain that William Goldman, who won an Academy Award for screenwriting *Butch Cassidy and the Sundance Kid,* was a fan of the play.

In 1967, William Goldman, who let me call him Bill, came up with a most original idea for a book on the theater. He called it *The Season,* and he chose a half dozen shows that were slated to open that season and asked the producers to allow him to attend and write about the first read-through of their play, their first runthrough, the first paid preview, the first out-of-town opening, and finally the Broadway premiere. Our play was one he had chosen. He made two or three unscheduled visits, and when I asked him why the extra visits, he said, "Your show makes me laugh—and I enjoy laughing."

When Bill was in Boston, he interviewed me in my suite at the Ritz. He asked me about the problems I encountered doing double duty as playwright and director. I admitted to having a couple of gut-churning sessions with two members of the cast recently, that were rather loud and heated, and this was, as Jackie Mason would say, "not in my nature." Bill remarked that I seemed to be remarkably calm and centered, considering the pressure I was under. He asked what I did to relieve tension. I had no answer.

Bill included in his chapter on *Something Different* an observation he made on leaving my suite. After commenting how well I was handling the stress of the job, he noticed me sticking out my tongue and examining it in the hall mirror and asked what was wrong.

"I think I burned my tongue," I said, "but I don't know how. I haven't had any hot coffee or soup. It might be a vitamin A deficiency."

"Or"—he said smiling—"unreleased tension that you stored in your tongue."

I knew his diagnosis was right, but for the record, since Boston, my tongue has never again tensed up.

One more digression, and then on to the Big Apple. I think it is unfair to mention that I had problems with two of the cast members, that is, unfair to the actors, at whom I didn't yell. I have shouted at only three actors in my career as a director, and I was wrong to lose control in all three cases. The only shabby excuse I can offer is that I yelled to release the pressure in my tense tongue before it exploded in my mouth and blew out my teeth. The two hapless victims of my wrath in *Something Different* were Linda Lavin, one of the theater's most gifted actresses, a Tony Award–winner for her performance in Neil Simon's *Brighton Beach Memoirs,* and the late Claudia McNeil, who thrilled us as Sidney Poitier's mama in *Raisin in the Sun.* The third was Mary Tyler Moore, to whom I have already apologized in an earlier chapter.

I don't think that there is a playwright extant who does not blame the drama critics' cruel and wrongheaded reviews for their play's being a flop. Here now is my sad but true tale of critics and their power to kill, or in my case, to maim. If I were to title my tale of sour grapes, it would be, "Shut up, Walter Kerr, You're Too Late!"

Most playwrights will tell you that opening-night audiences are traditionally not as demonstrative as a regular audience. Many opening-night seats are filled by relatives and friends, who are rooting for you and are looking around to see how well the play is being received by other friends. The more sophisticated well-wishers are also keeping an eye on the critics. My perceptive daughter, Annie, who had seen the play many times during its Boston run and had given it a glowing review, was seated in the third row. During the first intermission, she came to me and complained about the man who was seated next to her.

"He smells of liquor and is distracting everyone around him. Dad, not only did he come in after the curtain went up but he fell fast asleep as soon as he sat down," Annie reported angrily, "and he's snored during the whole act! Someone should wake up that drunk and ask him to leave!"

"Honey, we can't," I explained, "that drunk is John Chapman, the *New York Daily News* drama critic!"

I had heard that Mr. Chapman often imbibed before

reviewing a show but seemed to be able to do his job well enough to remain the newspaper's first-line critic. I don't know what filtered into his consciousness, but he gave *Something Different* one of the shortest and most dismissive reviews in history. I think he did mention that the audience seemed to be having a good time, but he had no idea why.

I do not mean to imply that our show failed because of Mr. Chapman's review. The situation then, as applied to criticism, is ostensibly the same now. The only review that can make or break a show is the one offered by the critic of *The New York Times*—and herein lies the rub. Walter Kerr, the venerable and distinguished *Times* critic for two decades, had that week decided to semiretire, and became the editor of the paper's Sunday Drama Section. Stepping into Mr. Kerr's shoes was Clive Barnes, an intelligent and decent man, who would be reviewing his very first play as a drama critic. Until this eventful night, Mr. Barnes had been the newspaper's dance critic.

His review of *Something Different* was of a proper length and quite literate but it was apparent that he did not understand the play or its references. I attribute this to his having been born and bred in England and having no interest in, or knowledge of, how a Bronx-bred neurotic Jewish playwright thinks, talks, or behaves. His review was what Manny Azenberg called a nonreview. It listed the actors, praised some of them, and offered the readers the kind of information about the play that would not send them running to the box office.

Now comes the second chorus of my sad song. The audience reaction was everything we hoped for but sadly the size of the audiences was not. It seems that good word of mouth depends on there being enough mouths in the audience to spread the good words. In spite of excellent reviews in the

New York Post, Variety, the Newhouse newspapers and practically all of the radio and TV critics, nobody was dashing to our box office; some ambled there but not enough.

(Less than two minutes ago, I looked for and found dog-eared copies of those reviews, and if my publisher doesn't think I'm being too defensive, tasteless, or self-aggrandizing, I am tempted to photocopy them and add them to the end of this diatribe—it is getting to be that, isn't it?)

On the third Sunday after our opening, something happened that caused all four of our producers, our stars, and me to call each other in case we had not read Walter Kerr's rave review in the Sunday *Times*. Had Walter Kerr's review come out the morning after opening night, we might have lasted more than the three months we did.

When I heard of our show closing after a hundred performances, I took solace in knowing that John Barrymore's acclaimed performance of Hamlet had closed after one hundred performances, and Richard Burton's Hamlet closed after one hundred and one. Burton insisted on doing that one extra performance. One-upping the great Barrymore was a triumph of sorts. Such is the ego of us folk in show biz.

Besides the brilliant comic performances of Bob Dishy and the rest of the talented cast, there are three incidents related to the show that tickle my fancy and feed my ego—and who among us doesn't enjoy being tickled and fed?

Ego feeder number one: This was related to me by Gabe Dell. During a curtain call, a little old man ran toward the stage waving his hands and shouting angrily at the audience to stop applauding. Gabe said that he was ready to jump off the stage and subdue the maniac when he realized that the little old man was Groucho Marx, who, without his painted-on mustache, looked like any little old man. The audience had no idea it was Groucho until they heard him speak. He asked the audience if they agreed that *Something Different* was the funniest show they had ever seen. When they applauded, he told them that it was their responsibility to keep the show running by stopping people in the street and spreading the word.

Just recently, another little old man who was seated next to Groucho that night confirmed the story. That other little old man, thirty-five years ago, was Groucho's young son, author and playwright Arthur Marx.

Ego Feeder number two: The lovely, talented actress Joan Hackett came up to me at a restaurant, introduced herself, and proceeded to tell me about having a matinee ticket for *Something Different*. For fear of being late, she had rushed to the theater from her dance class without changing out of her leotards. She told about a line and a piece of business that Bob Dishy did that made her laugh so hard that what she feared might happen did happen.

"I peed in my leotards," she admitted, "and couldn't stop! I sat through the whole show with water squishing in my Capezios."

What the ad men could have done with that! *Something Different* has them rolling in the aisles and peeing in their leotards!

Ego feeder number three: About four or five years after the show closed, I found myself in London with my wife when a man, who heard my name, asked if I was the Reiner who had written "that terribly amusing play with the four sets of identical twins."

(Yes, four sets, It's explained at the end of the play—get a copy from Samuel French, Inc., if you must know why four sets.)

I remember saying, "You saw my play? You're a member of a very exclusive group." I really was excited that someone from another continent, a gentleman who spoke with the most British of British accents, knew about my play. I couldn't let him go without debriefing him. He might have more to say about "that terribly amusing play."

"Did you like the play?" I asked, fishing for a compliment.

He smiled at me, bent his head forward, pointed to a spot on his forehead, and, with a Rex Harrison lilt, asked, "Do you see this?"

I looked closely and saw a tiny scar. "The scar?" I asked.

"Somewhere in the first act," he began, ignoring my question, "when the heavyset black woman and the author are discussing his play, I found her critique of Bud's play to be so uproariously funny that I burst out laughing. Involuntarily, to be sure, my head flew forward and I gashed my forehead on the seat in front of me. I bled like a stuck pig."

"What did you do?" I asked, loving the story.

"Pressed my hankie on the wound to stop the flow. Kept it there for the remainder of the show. Doctor put in a stitch or two," he said, pointing to the scar. "Did a good job, don't you think?"

When I think about these incidents, and I *do* think about them, I feel a sense of fulfillment. What better testament to my talent than knowing that I have the ability to make sophisticated theatergoers laugh until they pee and bleed!

16

Mickey Rooney, 99.99% Perfect

While writing the screenplay for *The Comic,* my friend and collaborator Aaron Rubin and I often remarked how lucky we were that Dick Van Dyke, who in the history of television, was the finest all-around performer to ever grace a situation comedy, signed on to play the role of Billy Bright. It was not just that Dick Van Dyke was the perfect actor to play the part of a fictional silent-movie comedian, he was the only actor for it. Dick so admired the great silent movie comedians Buster Keaton, Stan Laurel, Oliver Hardy, and Charles Chaplin that he bemoaned the fact that he was born forty years too late to be a part of their era. I heard Dick voicing this wish often during the time we spent together in the '60s. I believe, if Mephistopheles popped in on Dick and offered him a chance to sell his soul for the chance to work in those old black-and-white comedies, he would think long and hard before refusing.

Without resorting to satanic help, our good luck continued. The brilliant Mickey Rooney agreed to play the role of Billy Bright's best friend, Cockeye. In the late '30s and early

'40s Mickey Rooney was the number-one box-office draw for three consecutive years and was considered to be Hollywood's most versatile and bankable star. There was nothing he couldn't do, and whatever he did, he did brilliantly. He could sing, dance, compose songs, play the piano, perform flamboyant drum solos, strum a mean banjo, and effectively play both comedic and dramatic roles. Never has there been a happier pair of producer-writers than Aaron and I. We had our dream cast, Dick Van Dyke, Mickey Rooney, and the beautiful and vivacious Broadway singing star Michelle Lee as Dick's co-star. This would be my second film-directing job. Being responsible for a major motion picture that was budgeted for $3 million, three times the amount I had spent on my first film, *Enter Laughing*, was a little unsettling. I was also concerned about how a bona-fide film legend would take to being directed by a nervous, insecure neophyte. Why would he do what I suggested? Why should he? Well, he didn't! On our first day of rehearsal, my film legend balked at doing a simple thing that I politely asked him to do.

"I'm sorry, Mr. Reiner," he demurred, "but I'm afraid I can't do what you're asking!"

At first, I assumed he was joking as he had a big grin on his face—and his addressing me as Mr. Reiner had a playful ring to it. Now, as I've said, Mr. Rooney was contracted to play a character called Cockeye, loosely based on the silent film comedian Ben Turpin. Mr. Turpin, besides being a very able comedian, was also very cross-eyed. Today you do see women with Bette Davis eyes, but thanks to modern surgical procedures, you will rarely see anyone with Ben Turpin eyes. In the days of political incorrectness, it was not uncommon to hear some cruel kid yell out, "Hey, Cockeye, why don't ya look where yer goin'?"

Back then, laughing at physical afflictions was not only acceptable but profitable to the studio and the afflicted one. Ben Turpin was paid handsomely to produce and star in dozens of silent comedies. Oh, to be young, talented, and cross-eyed!

"Mickey," I explained, "I am aware how difficult it is to act with your eyes crossed! That's why I asked how long you can keep them crossed before it becomes uncomfortable."

I went on to assure him that I was planning for him not to have to cross his eyes for the long shots or the over-the-shoulder shots, and I would be very judicious about the angles I chose for scenes he was in. I impressed on him that tight close-ups were a must to establish his crossed eyes. I promised to be very solicitous of his comfort and would not require him to keep them crossed longer than absolutely necessary.

Mickey listened and then calmly explained why he balked.

"Carl, I cannot cross my eyes," he said, apologetically, "I have *never* been able to cross my eyes. I wish I could, but I can't! I don't know why—maybe it's because my mother told me that if I cross my eyes, they'll stay that way—sorry."

I didn't know how to react. I looked to Aaron and Dick and breathed a sigh of relief, they had big, smiles on their faces. Those funsters were in on the big practical joke Mickey was playing on his director!

"Okay, you got me, Mickey," I said, "you are such a damn good actor that, for a second, I believed you. You son-of-gun, you scared the shit out of me!"

Mickey quickly convinced us that he wasn't trying to scare the shit out of me but really could not cross his eyes. Now, this was something I would not accept, and I did not panic. I have nowhere near the talent or versatility of this great actor, but I do have the ability to cross my eyes, and, more importantly, to teach others how to cross theirs. In my time I have successfully taught my son the Director, my daughter the Poet, and my son the Artist, (i.e Rob, Annie, and Lucas) how to cross their beautiful blue eyes. I have even instructed my Academy Award–winning friend, Anne Bancroft, who was able to cross her eyes beautifully but wanted to learn how to uncross them one eye at a time, a technique developed by the master comic Harry Ritz and appropriated by me when I was sixteen. Using this Ritz refinement, Ms. Bancroft got a huge laugh uncrossing her crossed eyes in Mel Brooks's film *The Silent Movie*. I felt confident that I would be able to teach the most coordinated human being on earth how to cross his eyes. I made it clear to him that, in order to play Cockeye, it was absolutely essential for him to master this technique.

"Hey, to make it easy on everyone," he suggested, excitedly, "why don't we just change the character's name? Instead of Cockeye, we call him Cocky—I'll *play* him cocky, like Jack Oakie! He gets big laugh playing cocky—cocky's good for comedy—or Shorty! How about Shorty? Acting short is a snap for me—best thing I do. Let's go with Shorty!"

I explained that having a cross-eyed comic in the film was a quick brushstroke that would evoke the silent movie era.

"Right," Mickey argued, "but *short* is a better brushstroke—lots of shorties in silent films. Charlie Chaplin, the Little Tramp! Can't beat that for a brushstroke—you know he and I are about the same size. Or how about Fatty, like Fatty Arbuckle! I'll wear a fat suit, it'll be hilarious," he rattled on, "and his once being tried on a morals charge for the thing he did with that girl in a hotel room—it'll add dimension to his character—or maybe not—naw, you're right, too depressing for a comedy."

After talking himself in and out of alternate nicknames, he

reluctantly agreed to let me try teaching him how to cross his eyes.

"Just relax and look straight ahead," I instructed, "now, without moving your head—look up at the ceiling."

Mickey followed my two directions perfectly, and I was heartened.

"Good, good," I encouraged, "now, without moving, look at the bridge of your nose."

Mickey tried looking at the bridge of his nose—but his eyes, instead of turning inward, looked in the same direction.

"I told you I couldn't do it," he moaned.

"You will," I promised, "I have never failed."

"Until you met the Mick!" he warned. "Sorry to ruin your record!"

"I won't let you. Now, just relax and watch me. First, I open my eyes wide," I said, demonstrating, "then I take my index finger and point it at my forehead. Notice how I keep my finger at a right angle to my face. Now, I am staring at the tip of my finger and I keep staring at it as I bring it closer and closer to the bridge of my nose until it touches! And . . . voilà, my eyes are crossed! I now see two Mickey Rooneys, and both of you are out of focus."

Mickey applauded my effort and agreed to try again. He crossed his fingers and said he hoped his eyes would too, but after struggling mightily and failing, he gave up. He apologized for his ineptitude and suggested that we look for another actor. Neither Aaron nor I nor Mike Frankovich, the studio head, would hear of it. There was no other actor who could bring to the role and to the project what Mickey could.

At a high-level production meeting, someone suggested something that we all jumped at. The perfect solution—a prosthesis! A thin glass right eye with the pupil set in the left corner and placed over Mickey's right eye. All Mickey had to do to get the cross-eyed effect, would be to look to the right when talking to someone. We had two weeks of rehearsals before starting principal photography, and we were assured by people who knew, that there was ample time to get the impression of Mickey's right eye and create the glass one. The day before the filming started, an artisan named Maurice unveiled his creation. We ooohed and ahhhed as if we were viewing the Kohinoor diamond.

That first time Mickey Rooney walked onto the set wearing his "eye" we burst into applause. The Cockeye character we all had envisioned stood there glaring at us. We were all heartened to see how natural the eye looked and, a moment later, completely disheartened.

"Maurice, you sonovabitch," Mickey exploded, *"get this friggin' boulder out of my eye! Now!!"*

That is when we learned about Mickey Rooney's sensitivities and allergies. Putting any foreign substance in his eye caused him great pain and serious eye inflammation. What should have been a joyous first day of work with the great Mickey Rooney turned out to be a nightmare for all, especially the Mick. We rescheduled the day's work and devised a special routine for the days that Mickey was required to put "the boulder" in his eye. An eye doctor was hired to be on the set anytime Mickey worked, and the doctor never put in the prosthetic eye until the camera and sound were rolling and the scene number slated. As soon as the scene was over and I yelled "Cut," the doctor rushed in and removed the eye while the pained, tortured star cursed the doctor, the eye, Columbia Pictures, and all of us who worked for the company. This routine would be repeated for every take of every scene that Cockeye was in. Every night Mickey would go home with a headache but happy to be where no one would be putting their fingers in his eyes.

Midway in the filming, Mickey started to have fun. His right eye was still inflamed and paining him but being the superb actor he was, he acted as if it weren't. Between takes, Mickey would make up elaborate story lines for imaginary film projects he claimed to be developing. He ad-libbed dozens of these stories and he would keep talking right up to the time the doctor popped in his cocked eye and I yelled "Action!" Once, while waiting for a scene to start, I saw Mickey pantomiming a jockey in the final stretch, whipping his horse and making vocal sound effects of hoofbeats while imitating the excited delivery of the track announcer describing "the race of the century." Stanislavski, who wrote *An Actor Prepares*, advised actors, before starting a scene, to ask the director for a minute or two to get into character. After I shouted "Action!" it took a nanosecond for Mickey to stop his rapid-fire track announcing and morph into a slow-speaking, caring Cockeye who tearfully exhorts his drunken friend Billy to "lay off the booze!"

Mickey Rooney became so fond of the cast and crew that he often paid visits to the set even when he was not scheduled to work. But work he did. In between takes, he entertained everyone, inventing new and wilder screenplays, doing dozens of characters and vocal sound effects. It was hard for any of us to tell this sweet madman that he had to stop because we were ready to shoot. Often we didn't tell him, thus penalizing ourselves for our timidity by losing time and money. I did manage to come up with a solution. Mickey once told me that he loved marching to band music. Whenever he heard a marching band, he could not resist strutting and prancing about like a drum major. He demonstrated it once by singing "Stars and Stripes Forever," strutting about the stage, and then marching right out the studio door. The following day, I hired a three-piece band, a drum, a trumpet, and a saxophone, and I made a deal with Mickey. I told him that he was welcome to entertain the cast and crew between takes, but when he heard the marching band play, he was to start marching and strut his way out of the studio. We kept the three-piece marching band on salary and thereby managed to finish *The Comic* on time and on budget.

The Comic was what many consider a *succès d'estime*, a French term for "classy, but it won't make a lot of money." They were right!

17

Two Weird Coincidences

I am pleased to offer you these weird coincidences. For a while, I feared that they might never see the light of your bed lamp. They were previously a part of the chapter *A Purse Is Not a Pocket Book,* but a powerful associate, whom I allow to whisper in my ear, felt they were digressions, entertaining but perhaps also confusing to readers who dislike disconnected connectives. Personally, I love digressions, especially when the subject to which the person is digressing is at least as interesting as the subject from which the digresser has digressed. And I know I am not the only one who feels this way. I learned recently from my learned friend David Chasman that no lesser a man than Herodotus, who lived 2,500 years ago, was a digressing fool. In his honor, and as a bonus to you, I will describe a coincidence that was formerly a digression that scared the piss out of me when I was eighteen and a resident actor at the Rochester Summer Theater in Avon, New York.

One evening after dinner the members of our company were stretched out in the front parlor of the rooming house we called home and were listening to a radio program called *Professor Quiz*. Professor Quiz would shove a microphone at a member of the studio audience and ask a random question that, if answered correctly, could be worth as much as ten dollars, which for my folks, was half a month's rent. I had just come from my room, and as I walked to the front door, I announced confidently, "The answer to the next question is Mickey Cochrane!" I stopped and stared open-mouthed at the radio when I heard the professor ask, "For ten dollars, sir, can you tell me the name of the catcher for the Detroit Tigers?"

"Mickey Cochrane!" the man shouted out, and the room became eerily silent. No one believed me when I said that it was a stab in the dark and that I was as shocked as they were. It scared the hell out of me. I thought I had developed occult powers.

Well, if I had occult powers at eighteen, then I lost them somewhere along the way. Today, on *Jeopardy,* even when Alex Trebek gives us the correct answers, I have trouble coming up with the questions.

THE SECOND WEIRD COINCIDENCE

Lucas, our youngest child, a most talented artist, a shoo-in selection for the Baseball Hall of Fame had he elected to continue playing baseball, and one of the best sons, fathers, husbands, and human beings I know, was curious about his grandfather, my father. He phoned me one afternoon to ask if I could tell him a little about the town in the Austro-Hungarian Empire where my father was born. He asked how to spell the name of the town, and I said that I thought it was C-H-E-R-N-O-W-I-T-Z but was not sure. He wanted to know its exact spelling for the family tree he and his wife, Maud, were working on. While telling him that I would try to find out more about the town, the doorbell rang and I asked Luke to hold on while I went to see who it was. It was the mailman with a package that I opened on my way back to the phone. In it was a book, a most extraordinary book, *Faith, Hope and Charity,* by Arthur Spitzer.

"Luke," I said, into the phone, "the spelling I gave you is not correct—it's spelled, C-Z-E-R-N-O-W-I-T-Z, not C-*H*. . . ."

I then continued to give him information about the history of the town, when and how, after being annexed by Germany, it got to be part of Romania. I went on until Luke stopped me.

"Hey, Dad, where are you getting all this information?"

"From this book on Czernowitz," I said, calmly. "It just arrived in the mail."

I couldn't hold back any longer, and told him what had just happened. He thought I was kidding him. What a fantastic, unbelievable, mind-boggling coincidence we had just shared. What are the odds that I would get this obscure information in the mail at just the moment my son asked for it? A quintillion to one would be my guess. Now, for a partial explanation:

Three years earlier, I met a gentleman at a party who heard me say that my father was born in Czernowitz. He excitedly informed me that he was born in Czernowitz and was going to write a book about his life there before World War II and after the Nazi invasion. I gave him my address, and he promised that if his book was ever published, he would send me a copy. It took three years to arrive, but for Luke and me it was right on time!

18

Take It from the Ten-Letter Word!

The novel *Where's Poppa?* written by Robert Klane was brought to my attention by my literary agent, Mike Zimring. He thought it hilariously funny and wondered if I might be interested in directing the film that the author was in the process of writing. After belly-laughing my way through the book, I concurred that it was absolutely hilarious and completely insane to think that anyone could fashion a movie from this strange, scatological, Oedipal-driven novel—and that is why I agreed to do it. It was a challenge to make a movie that I had no idea how to do, a challenge I was eager to take on—as were the producers Jerry Tokofsky and Marvin Worth, their star, George Segal, and United Artists' David Picker, who had agreed to finance the risky venture.

Input from the producing-directing team, and especially from George Segal, whose insightful suggestions about cutting and rearranging scenes, helped Bob Klane to whip the final draft into shape. In record-breaking time, Bob delivered a taut, funny, and neatly typed screenplay. He was the best author-typist I have ever encountered, and because of his

148

taut, funny, neat screenplay we secured the services of Ruth Gordon, who agreed to play Mrs. Hockheiser, mother to George Segal's Gordon Hockheiser.

I was aware that we were operating on a minimal budget, but I did not realize how minimal until we flew to New York to search for locations. We toured the city in the dead of winter, riding about in a rattling car of indeterminate make and vintage. It had no heater, one window that could not be closed, and brakes that needed aggressive pumping to stop. In spite of the inconveniences, we enthusiastically went about securing locations, hiring actors, and behaving as if we were not working for minimal salaries and no perks.

Somehow, our budget constraints did not inhibit our ability to recruit an excellent cast of actors. George invited me to see his friend Ron Liebman in an off-Broadway play, and I was impressed by his extraordinary performance.

"George," I whispered, "he'd be perfect to play your brother, if he were older."

"He could be," George whispered back, "if he took off his toupee."

Surprisingly, I did not know he was wearing one.

"Great, tell him to lose the rug, and he's got the part!"

"You tell him," George replied, "he's never been seen without it."

"Has he ever been in a big Hollywood movie?" I asked. "It might be an incentive."

I don't remember which of us broached the subject of his doing the part toupeeless, but after reading the script and realizing what a juicy part he was being offered, young, virile Ron Liebman, who had never been in a movie, agreed to stow his hairpiece and play a balding, older man.

Having toiled half my life as an actor, I prefer to cast a

film by offering the job to someone I know would be right for the role, rather than having many actors read for the same part. For the role of Louise, Gordon Hockheiser's love, I asked the casting director Marian Dougherty to invite no more than three actresses who, she felt, would be perfect for the part—and she did. I met with three wonderfully talented and beautiful actresses, Diane Keaton, Trish Van Devere, and Bernadette Peters, two of whom it pained me to reject. The pain was relieved when, ten years later, I had the opportunity to make amends by offering the wondrous Bernadette Peters, a former "rejectee," the part of Marie, Steve Martin's girlfriend, in *The Jerk*.

Diane Keaton, the other perfect actress whom I didn't hire, had somehow managed to get over her disappointment and go on to win an Oscar. She has since become a director and asked me to audition for an acting role in her film *Hanging Up,* and evened our score by rejecting me and wisely choosing Walter Matthau. I carry on as do Diane and Bernadette and all actors who suffer rejection.

When Paul Sorvino came to read for the part of the manager/owner of Gus and Grace's home for old people, he was contemplating a return to the acting profession. Paul had been a struggling actor, but at this juncture was a successful advertising executive who was frustrated and demonstrably unhappy. Paul's wife insisted that life in their home would be a lot more fun were he working in the profession he loved. On his way to bigger and better things, among them helping to raise his award-winning daughter, Mira, Paul worked for me again, doing a scathingly funny satire of an evangelical preacher in *Oh God!*

I had no trouble casting twenty-two-year-old Rob Reiner as the angry anti-Vietnam-war activist. In the courtroom scene, the character shouts scatological invectives at the general, played by everyone's favorite character actor Barnard Hughes.

The general, in one scene, has just gleefully testified that he had machine-gunned a whole platoon of Vietcong soldiers, and that one soldier's body, sawed in half by his bullets, had fallen over, "and if I had yelled 'Forward march,' those scrawny little legs would have walked over by themselves." I tell you all this to make you understand that the "obscene" language Bob Klane had chosen for the young activist to shout was appropriate. The scene was shot in a real court-house, in a real New York borough, Brooklyn. It was a complicated scene to shoot, as all courtroom scenes are, requiring many camera setups for the many angles needed to edit the scene effectively. George Segal was questioning the general while the judge, Bill LeMassena, a *Call Me Mister* alumnus, and the courtroom spectators, were all staring openmouthed at the general's gruesome recounting of the battle. At the height of the general's graphic description, the antiwar activist loses control, vaults the defense table, and comes after the general, shouting the ten-letter word "Cocksucker!!!"

After that very first take, my assistant director, Norman Cohen, informed me that the camera didn't get a clean shot of the action and asked that we do another take right away. Being on a tight schedule, and knowing we only had the courtroom for one day, I was not aware that when I shouted, "Okay, Rob, we're going do it from where you yell, 'Cock-sucker,'" I was asking my son to say the very word that Lenny Bruce had been arrested and incarcerated for using six months earlier! What kind of father was I?!

The scene was shot four or five times, and each time Rob vaulted the table and shouted the actionable ten-letter word, a couple of burly uniformed policemen would grab him and drag him kicking and screaming from the courtroom as he continued to rail louder and louder against the horrors of the unjust war. I had no trouble embracing the sentiment, but that it was delivered in a wild, satiric comedy about a dutiful, guilt-ridden son and his seemingly dotty mother was surreal and sobering.

Two other memories about the shooting of *Where's Poppa,* bubble up from time to time. One of them was a confrontation I had with Ruth Gordon. Miss Gordon, who invited me to call her Ruth the first day we met, was an actress and playwright of talent and renown. The incident took place on the first day of rehearsal. We were in the dining room set that was built on one of the stages of the Twentieth Century Fox New York studios on Eleventh Avenue. The scene required Ruth Gordon's character to fall asleep in a dish of mashed potatoes while having dinner with her son and his new girlfriend, Louise. When Ruth stopped the scene to complain that there was something in the script that she did not like, I assumed she was referring to the previous scene in which she showed Louise the first two knuckles of her pinky and said that her son's penis was no bigger than that, but I was wrong. What Miss Gordon objected to was falling asleep in the mashed potatoes.

"I don't think it's funny," she said simply.

"I think it is," I said smiling. "And if it isn't, I guarantee it will not be in the final cut."

"I would prefer we didn't shoot it."

"But we've all read it, and nobody's objected to it."

"Well, I'm objecting now!"

When the discussion started, George Segal was standing beside me, and I felt that I had his support. As the exchanges between Miss Gordon and myself became more pointed, I could feel an impasse coming. I could also feel George physically backing away. When I turned, looking for support, he was gone. He had quietly vanished into the darkened stage, and he was right to leave it to Ruth and me to come to an accommodation, and we did.

"I refuse to do the scene the way it is written," she said, pausing dramatically, then adding forcefully, "unless the director orders me to."

She looked at me and waited for my response.

"Ruth," I said, feigning strength and resolve, "I order you to do the scene as written."

I don't know if Ruth Gordon was testing me to see if I had the "stuff" to direct or faith in my convictions but whatever her motive, those were the last contentious words we had. We had a lovely time working and promoting the film together.

If you remember the film, you probably think that Ruth Gordon prevailed, because the scene was not as I described it. In rehearsals we found that we could get two or three extra laughs if Gordon, to discourage his mother from remaining at the table, would, when serving her, give her just a dollop of the mashed potatoes and one green pea, then place the serving plates out of her reach. Instead of her head falling into a mound of potatoes, she fell asleep on a dollop of potato, saving both time and money. No redoing Ruth's makeup and no remashing of potatoes.

There is a law in New York that forbids a movie company from filming people running around their city in the nude. An important scene in *Where's Poppa?* required Sid, Ron Liebman's character to run across a street stark naked, his clothes having been stolen by a playful bunch of Central Park muggers. The police had been with us all day, helping with traffic and crowd control, and were very pleasant and cooperative. The sergeant in charge knew about the scene, and we assured him that, if we ever got to the scene that night, Ron would be wearing boxer shorts. To avoid there being spectators watching us shoot the scene, we shut down at midnight and did not fire up the lights until three in the morning, seconds before Ron was to dash across street. With his tush facing the camera, he was to run into the apartment building at Sixty-fifth Street and Central Park West, the building in which George Segal actually lived. Five seconds before we lit up the street, it was deserted, and two seconds before we rolled the cameras, hundreds of people appeared miraculously from the ether, to see what was going on. The police sergeant was at my elbow when I yelled "Action!" We had two cameras rolling and got what we wanted in one take.

"Hey, Mr. Reiner," the officer asked politely, "that actor was bare-ass naked—did you know that actor was going to be naked?"

"No, dammit, I didn't," I shouted, feigning anger, "he was supposed to be wearing boxers. Norman!" I called to my assistant, "Who the hell told Ron he could take off the boxers?"

"Not me!" he answered innocently. "Probably Ron's idea, you know these method actors."

"You planning to shoot it again?" the sergeant asked.

"No, sir, everybody is pooped," I said, disappointed, "we'll just live without the damn shot. All right, Norman," I shouted, "that's a wrap!"

"See that it is a wrap!" the officer ordered.

I smiled at the sergeant, and the sergeant smiled back. He knew I was lying and would use the nude shot, and I knew he knew and was grateful for his appreciation of the creative process. We all gained from the sergeant's kindness. The author's work was respected, the audience got an extra laugh, and those who fancy a well-toned buttock got a good look at one.

Of the many pleasures working at New York's Twentieth Century Fox Studios, the one that George Segal and I enjoyed most, was the al fresco dining on Eleventh Avenue. On more than one occasion we left the studio by the back door, strolled a short distance, to our favorite curbside vendor, and ordered a couple of Sabrett hot dogs with mustard and sauerkraut.

Again I am proud to report, we finished our movie on time and miraculously on budget. We returned to California where, with my trusted editor-friend, Bud Molin, who worked with me for five years on *The Dick Van Dyke Show* and on all but two of my fifteen films, we made *Where's Poppa?* ready for previews in a relatively short time.

We screened it for the United Artists executives and a couple of our friends, who all genuinely loved what they saw. Mel Brooks concurred and said that he could not believe we dared to make a movie he should have made. The UA executives, fresh from this successful screening, had such faith in the film's potential that they opted to present not just a short trailer of their new product to the National Alliance of Theater Owners' convention in Miami Beach, as other studios were going to do, but to screen the entire film. It was a gamble, but one they felt comfortable taking.

The audience reaction was definite and measurable. It was this first reaction that was, in good part, responsible for the ultimate place that *Where's Poppa?* holds in film history.

Of all the films I have directed, only *Where's Poppa?* is universally acknowledged as a cult classic. A cult classic, as you may know, is a film that was seen by a small minority of the world's filmgoers, who insist that it is one of the greatest, most daring, and innovative moving pictures ever made. Whenever two or more cult members meet, they will quote dialogue from the classic and agree that "the film was ahead of its time." To be designated a genuine cult classic, it is of primary importance that the film fail to earn back the cost of making, marketing, and distributing it. *Where's Poppa?* was made in 1969 for a little over $1 million. According to the last distribution statements I saw, it will not break even until it earns another $650,000.

That fateful evening in Miami Beach, more than half the audience, led by the older, conservative, outraged wives of the theater owners, walked out, en masse, mumbling and grousing as they went. Those who found the film hilariously funny were greatly outnumbered by the humorless folk, who found it deeply disgusting. The sad fact is that many millions, who might have loved the film, were scared off by the vehement badmouthing of its detractors. However, those millions, by renting a copy of *Where's Poppa?* still have an opportunity to judge for themselves who is right and who is humorless. If there are enough of you, it is not impossible to hope that *Where's Poppa?* will make new fans and enough new income to lose its standing as a cult classic.

19

Billy Wilder's Bratwurst

Estelle and I were fortunate to have been able to spend fifteen idyllic summers vacationing in our small house in the south of France. There in our modest backyard we cultivated tomatoes that tasted like real tomatoes—the kind they sold in the Bronx in the 1930s, the kind my mother bought from Abe, our neighborhood vegetable man who my mother fixed up with her stout cousin, Helen—a successful matchmaking that ensured my mother bringing home the freshest vegetables and the plumpest fruit. Besides cultivating real tomatoes during those carefree étés in France, we cultivated real friends, who are still in our lives. One such friend is central to this story, and if, because of the title, you guessed Billy Wilder, you guessed wrong. While in France, we never saw Mr. Wilder or anyone who resembled him. Among the half dozen people with whom we bonded was a couple whose hospitality helped make our days so special. To protect their privacy, I will call them Jim and Betty. Their real names are Arman and Corice, and as I think about it, Arman doesn't want his privacy protected, he being a world-renowned artist who loves and deserves his renown. His massive sculptures and brilliant paintings grace the squares and museums of the world's great cities. Corice is a beauty, a gourmet cook, a hostess in the Perle Mesta tradition, and if their children, Yasmine and Philippe, are any testament, a very good and caring mother. I am not sure how we met Corice and Arman, but I think it was through a mutual friend, who I will call Jeffrey Robinson, because he is an author of best-sellers who loves seeing his name in print. Jeffrey and I met years earlier when he was a young interviewer for the European edition of the *Herald Tribune* and I was a middle-aged interviewee. I'm not clear about why Arman and Corice invited us to lunch at their extraordinary home in Vence. It might have been because Jeff vouched for our character or because of my fame as a minor celebrity or my wife's ability to sing jazz—whatever it was, I'm happy it came about. Estelle and I saw things at Arman and Corice's home that we had never before seen anywhere, nor, I'll wager, have you, unless you've been to a house that has the following:

- fifteen hundred glistening chromium-plated washing-machine drums welded together, positioned to frame the roof and the front door of the house.
- a swimming pool, the access to which requires your strolling through a cavelike grotto where 2,500 telephones of various shapes, colors, and styles adorn every inch of the grotto's walls and ceiling.
- on the back patio, a two-ton bronze sculpture of a vintage Citroën auto, so badly pitted that one must surmise that it had been dredged up from the ocean's floor. Its title, *Future Archeological Find*, suggests that it had been resting there for hundreds of years.

- a fifteen-foot free-form pyramidlike sculpture that utilizes dozens of porcelain bathroom washbasins that becomes a soothing waterfall when the topmost basins' faucets are turned on.
- a living room with a club chair fashioned from hundreds of plastic paint-tube containers, a sofa constructed of wooden shoe lasts, and a fairly comfortable couch made up entirely of empty guitar cases.

I could cite a dozen more breathtakingly original examples of Arman's home art, but if I do that, we'll never get to Billy Wilder's bratwurst.

Throughout the years, Corice and Arman continued to wine and dine us lavishly in their homes in Vence and in New York, and sadly, we were never able to reciprocate in kind. Our guilt was almost unbearable, so when we learned they were coming to Los Angeles to attend the opening of Arman's new work at the Urbinati Gallery, we jumped at the chance to even the score—well, not exactly even it, but make it a tad less lopsided. We invited them to be the honored guests at a dinner party in our home to which we would invite some of our mutual friends and some who would become mutual. As an inducement, I added that it would be a home-cooked dinner. The moment the Armans accepted our invitation, Estelle started to worry about what to cook for this couple with the sophisticated palates, whose best friend was Roger Vergé, owner/chef of Le Moulin de Mougins. Estelle was not of a mind to compete with Roger Vergé or Corice who, at every one of her dinners, was invariably asked by one of her guests, often Estelle, "Can I get the recipe for that?"

What to make, what to make? We went through a list of the wonderful dishes we had eaten at the Armans' and knew that gourmet-wise we could not compete. We thought of all the great recipes Estelle had gotten from her mother, Minnie, like brisket of beef, chicken fricassee, or her lighter-than-air cheese blintzes, but decided that even though the Armans would think a good Jewish meal to be quaint, our relationship centered around our time together in France. Since we adored peasant-style French food and had never eaten any at their home, we opted to go with our all-time favorite peasant fare, choucroute Alsacienne!

On our four-day visit to Alsace, the choucroute capital of the word, I dined on their specialty for three consecutive dinners and one lunch. I was half the age I am now and had half of the knowledge of the damage that salt, fat, nitrates, and cholesterol can do to one's health, but that doesn't diminish my love for choucroute. Nowadays I rarely, if ever, eat it, but if I see it on a menu, I think long and hard before not ordering it. In the last twenty years, I've weakened but four times— well, five, if you count the totally unsatisfying version of it I ate on May 13, 2002, at a New York bistro. I left over more than half.

After deciding that choucroute Alsacienne was to be our main course, we went about gathering the many ingredients that would make our version singular but authentic. We started by making our own sauerkraut, using my grandmother's famous Old World recipe, which was handed down to my mother: "shredded cabbage and lots of salt water, to taste." We put these secret ingredients in a wide-necked, pottery crock, placed the crock in a warm place in the kitchen, and in four days, we uncovered the crock and said, "Phew, that stinks!" and knew that we had successfully created the base ingredient for our peasant dish. Now, of all the traditional meats that are piled atop the sauerkraut like slices of succulent ham and pork, German frankfurters, boiled ham hocks, to me the most important is the veal bratwurst. Bratwurst comes in all sizes and qualities, and if you've ever eaten a truly delicious one, you will never be satisfied with anything less. I was confident that we would hit a home run with our choucroute, because I knew where to get that perfect veal bratwurst. In 1969, while working at the Samuel Goldwyn Studios in Hollywood doing postproduction on *Where's Poppa?*, a film I had just directed, the great Billy Wilder, who had an office down the hall, invited me to join him for lunch. It was Jack Lemmon, I believe, who introduced us. After that initial meeting, whenever Billy and I passed each other in the hall, we'd exchange a few pleasant words about current films and how Jack Lemmon is really as nice as everyone says. It was at my lunch with Billy that I tasted that perfect bratwurst, and it was he who told me about his little German sausage maker on Third Street, off La Cienaga Boulevard. Well, his little German sausage maker became my sausage maker too, and I became his steady customer.

Since adhering to the low-fat, low-salt Pritikin diet, I had stopped shopping there. As I drove to the store, I thought about those plump white sausages in the display case, and was shocked to discover that hair dryers and beauty products had replaced the sausages. The little German sausage maker had retired! For the next few days, we made many calls to many butcher shops, literally scouring the countryside to find a worthy replacement.

After four or five disappointing taste tests, I was almost ready to settle for second best. I'm sure you're thinking, *Why didn't the idiot call Billy Wilder and ask him where he was buying his sausages?* Well, I did think of that, and also thought of a damned good reason why I should not call the man. At that time, Mr. Wilder was more or less retired and only did consulting work for friends and colleagues. Since I was a working director, I worried that he might think I was calling to offer him work as a consultant on a new project. If I were to tell him that I called to consult with him about bratwursts, he might think, *It's* Sunset Boulevard *and I'm Norma Desmond! That sonofabitch Cecil B. DeReiner doesn't want me, he wants my bratwurst!*

It was possible that he would not see it that way, but I couldn't take the chance of offending my idol. I remembered then that Billy Wilder had a steady lunch date with a mutual friend, Jay Weston, a film producer and the publisher of a popular and excellent restaurant guide. He would surely know if Mr. Wilder had found another purveyor of top bratwursts—and he did know! The farmer's market in the Beverly Center!

The dinner honoring Arman and Corice was a triumph! The choucroute Alsacienne was outstanding, the bratwursts being singled out for special praise, the conversation was witty, and the wine very fine, as Mel Brooks, our wine supplier, informed us each time he filled our glasses. He made us aware of the exact retail cost of each sip we took. The evening was everything we had envisioned, and it turned out to be one of my wife's most appreciated dinners—one of scores of appreciated dinners she has cooked in a lifetime of appreciated dinners.

The following night, all of our guests joined Arman's West Coast friends, collectors, and art lovers in attending the opening of his stunning new show. Hung around the gallery were huge canvases with bold slashes of vibrant-colored paint laid on heavily by large brushes that were left, glued to the canvases. He created another group of paintings by squeezing long rivulets of paint from their soft lead tubes and leaving the tubes on the canvas. Besides delighting collectors and afficionados on three continents, he is known to be the most sought-after customer by owners of art supply stores.

Soon after we arrived, I was shocked to see Billy Wilder stroll into the gallery. We looked at each other and, without a moment's hesitation—well, maybe *with* a moment's hesitation—I walked slowly to him, debating with myself about whether or not l'Affaire Bratwurst would be something Mr. Wilder might get a kick out of hearing.

"Hey, Billy," I said, shaking his hand, "what are you doing here?"

"What are *you* doing here?" he shot back. "I collect Armans, do you?"

"No." I said.

"Then buy something or get out!" he quipped.

I laughed and he smiled.

His smile told me that I could not keep the story of our dinner party from him.

"Say Billy," I said, tiptoeing into the tale, "you want to hear something funny?"

"How funny?" he asked. "I don't like to laugh on an empty stomach."

"That's funny," I said, chuckling.

"What, that I'm hungry?"

"No, that I was going to tell you about a dinner we just gave for Arman."

"That you didn't invite me to," he said, "what's amusing about that?"

"What's amusing is that I made choucroute and went to that sausage store to get those great bratwursts you told me about and—"

"—it became a beauty supply dump, I could have told you that," he snapped, looking at me strangely.

"I know, Billy," I said, smiling apologetically, "I was going to call you and ask you where you get your bratwursts now."

"And why didn't you?" he asked, looking at me strangely.

"Well." I giggled. "I called Jay Weston. . . . I thought that if I called you . . ."

"Well, it's good you didn't!"

"It is?"

"You bet." He sneered, grabbing my arm, his voice rising. *"If you had called me I would have become Gloria Swanson and thought that you called to offer me a job and this would have gotten me so damned excited that I would have made love to my wife—for no good reason!!"*

I laughed loud and hard, as did the everyone within earshot. Billy didn't laugh, but he did give me a wide and twinkly smile. Through the years, we both have related this story to our friends, and I'm sure if he were still around he wouldn't mind my telling it to you.

20

RRR Reiner, Shake My Hand and We Got a Deal!

When the aide to Charles Bluhdorn, the owner of Paramount Pictures, CEO of Gulf and Western, and the man who signed my paychecks, asked if my wife and I would care to spend Christmas with Mr. Bluhdorn and some friends at his home in the Dominican Republic, I hesitated, and then thought, *Why am I hesitating? Only a complete idiot would turn down this offer, and there being no real evidence that I am a complete one . . .*

Charles Bluhdorn could not have been more charming and gracious to us. Nowhere in his demeanor or behavior did I feel that I was talking to a multi-multibillionaire executive who had the power to fire me or have me executed. He introduced us to the other invitees, an eclectic group of talented, charming, witty, and accomplished people whose celebrity was a bit daunting. I felt completely out of my element with these people, who were so obviously *in* their element. My discomfort level dropped a bit when one of the guests, Jerzy Kosinski, the author of the classic *The Painted Bird* sought me out to chat about my television and film experiences. Jerzy

Kosinski's name is one of three or four celebrity names I plan to drop to help give this piece some journalistic accuracy. I had never met Mr. Bluhdorn, and I wondered why he was being so generous. Could it be that he'd heard about the positive reaction my new film received at a screening and was tossing me a little bonus? It was not till midway through our stay that I learned the real reason I had been invited.

That first morning, after breakfast, I was surprised to hear Mr. Bluhdorn shouting, "RRReiner, wanna go for a swim?" Without waiting for an answer, he ordered me to put on my bathing suit and meet him at the beach in five minutes. I wondered why he singled me out. I was curious about how he, a grade school dropout, who came to the United States from Poland with pennies in his pocket and no prospects, could manage, in a very short time, to become a scion of industry and the boss of me. So eager was I to have a one-on-one visit with him that I hurried to the beach sans cap, sunglasses, or sunblock. I thought of doubling back and retrieving them, but on hearing Mr. Bluhdorn shout, "RRRreiner, you're late!" I decided to manage without them.

Down at the shore, I spotted a shirtless Charles Bluhdorn sporting a floppy hat and sunglasses and standing knee-deep in the water.

"RRReiner," he shouted, splashing water on his face, "jump in, the water's perfect!"

Mr. Bluhdorn spoke with a Polish-German accent and rolled his r's as effectively as a Nazi drill sergeant. During my stay, those rolling r's rolled my way many times. He never just said my name, he shouted it. As I approached him, he tilted his head and stuck out his hand.

"RRReiner, shake my hand," he growled, "and we have a deal!"

I reflexively put out my hand but hesitated as I remembered a studio executive once say that my host regarded "a handshake to be more binding, morally, than a signature."

"Before I shake," I asked, stepping back, "can I ask what the deal is?"

"It's for a new picture I'm preparing," he said, offering his hand again, "shake and you've got yourself a deal!"

"A new picture," I asked politely, "can I read the script?"

"There is no script," he said, withdrawing his hand.

"Is there a treatment I could? . . ."

"There's no treatment," he barked, "just a story line."

"Can I read that?"

"No." He smiled. "It's in my head. I can tell it to you."

"When?"

"RRRight now! RRReady?"

I thought, *I am his guest, eating his food, making films for his company and wading in his ocean, how could I not be ready?*

"You're on, Mr. Bluhdorn," I said, enthusiastically.

At the same moment Mr. Bluhdorn set himself to begin, the sun, which had been hiding, peeped out from behind a cloud."

"Ah." I smiled. "A good omen!'

With Mr. Bluhdorn's first utterance, my smile froze.

"The title of the movie is," he announced dramatically, his hands sweeping the sky, *"Buffalo Bill Meets Adolf Hitler!"*

" '*Buffalo Bill Meets Adolf Hitler,*' " I asked, "it's a . . . what . . . a fantasy?"

"No, RRReiner, *a comedy!*" he explained impatiently, "*A comedy!* I need a comedy expert like you to write and direct it. Shake my hand, RRReiner, and you've got a deal."

Again I hesitated and he, realizing that I would not commit to the project without more details, started giving me details, many, many details, one more stupid than the other. Mr. Bluhdorn had positioned himself so that his back was to the blazing sun and my face was facing it. It beat down on my bald head mercilessly, and I stopped paying attention to the story and focused on how I might avoid a sunstroke and retina damage. I squinted, grimaced, and shaded my eyes with my hand, hoping Mr. Bluhdorn would notice and offer me his cap or sunglasses, but he was so totally concentrated on selling his silly story that he was unaware that my well-being was in jeopardy. I dared not interrupt my host-boss, but I knew I had to do something to protect my eyeballs. By taking baby steps and turning my body oh so slowly, I managed to inch my way to deeper, cooler water: Mr. Bluhdorn, intent on selling his movie, followed me, unaware that we were swapping positions.

After hearing how the story was set in "the wild, wild, wild West" and how Buffalo Bill was going to be the good guy and Adolf Hitler the villain, and how "Adolf and the Buffalo guy" would have a big gunfight over Eva Braun and her cattle land. I knew there would be no handshakes today. I thought, *Is this why he invited me here . . . to make a deal for this garbage?* And then I thought about what I would say when he finished and asked for my honest opinion. What could I possibly say, without compromising my integrity, that would not be cruel and insulting?

When, blessedly, he did finish, Mr. Bluhdorn had a huge grin on his face and looked at me expectantly. He didn't seem to know or care that I had maneuvered him to deeper water and had him facing the sun.

"So, RRReiner," he asked, smiling proudly, "what do you think? I want your honest opinion."

There it is, I thought, *a career-shaping dilemma!* How to critique his stupid story in a way that would minimize my chances of getting booted off the island and out of my offices at Paramount. I grinned back at him while shaking my head slowly back and forth. A slow head shake is a noncommittal comment that could mean "Boy, you sure are something!" or "You stink!" Using it gave me some extra time to decide between telling the truth or bullshitting, and very quickly I realized that the truth could set me free—free of further development sessions on this project.

"Mr. Bluhdorn," I said, acting thoughtful, "I think that *Buffalo Bill Meets Adolf Hitler* could well be—no, is—the worst idea for a comedy ever. It makes absolutely no sense and is just not funny. I can see no earthly reason why you would waste your time trying to develop this piece of sh—shhallowness." I paused, adding quietly, "If I were you, Mr. Bluhdorn, I'd dump it."

Mr. Bluhdorn stared at me long and hard while I attempted to act nonchalant.

"So, RRRReiner, you are telling me that my idea is stupid and not funny? *God damm it!*" he growled, "*that's what everybody tells me!* Well, thank you." He sighed. "You're the expert, so I guess I'll dump it, like you say."

I never expected this reaction to my critique, and wondered why he exerted all that energy describing something he knew stank? Maybe to test my honesty, or maybe check on my ability to judge material.

The day following our session at the seashore, Mr. Bluhdorn invited my wife and me to join him and his other guests on a tour of the island. We piled into one of five black limos and at every place of interest, while the cars were still rolling to a stop, black-suited bodyguards would appear from nowhere and open the doors for us. Two guards for each car. I noticed, after the next precision door opening, that three guards rode in the lead car and three in the last car, two carrying machine guns.

"Why the machine guns?" I asked our driver.

"Señor Bluhdorn loves *all* the people of this island," he explained simply, "but not *all* the people love Señor Bluhdorn."

The presence of machine guns was a little unsettling, but I shrugged it off. A host doesn't have a guest bumped off for telling him his story idea stinks.

My wife and I were properly impressed with an art colony Mr. Bluhdorn had built for young resident artists, and we told him so. After visiting a few of the island's points of interest, we were driven to the middle of a large, barren field. The moment the motorcade stopped, the bodyguards snapped those doors open and Mr. Bluhdorn excitedly ordered us to follow him. While hurrying alongside him and seeing no obvious point of interest in the barren field, I dared ask, "What are we doing here?"

"Going for a ride in a helicopter," he answered, peering up at the sky, "to give you a bird's-eye view of the whole island."

He had asked Estelle and me earlier if we would like to go for a helicopter ride, and we made it clear that we would not. I was about to remind him of that, when he stepped between us, took us by the hand as if we were two schoolchildren, and trotted us to a spot where, seconds later, a helicopter dropped from the sky and set down. It was at that moment, when he talked us into boarding "the safest copter ever built," that I understood how one becomes a billionaire. Set definite goals, own automatic weapons, and never take no for an answer. To give the devil his due, and he was a cute devil, we did enjoy our first, and still only, helicopter ride, and we thanked him for tricking us into it.

On the way back, Mr. Bluhdorn invited us to ride with him so he could continue his monomaniacal need for me to shake his hand.

"RRReiner," he exhorted, extending his hand as we settled in our seats, "shake and you got yourself a deal!"

"Not for *Buffalo Bill and*—?"

"No, no." He laughed. "No Bill, no Hitler. I'm serious, I want you to direct a great comedy."

"Does it have a title?"

"Yes, but I can't tell you that until we have a deal. RRReiner, if you want the deal, shake my hand!"

"I can't until you tell me something about—"

"All rrrright, tough guy," he growled, "I'll tell you one thing. The biggest star in the whole world has agreed to be in it!"

"And who might that be?"

"RRReiner, shake my hand and I'll tell you."

Variations of this conversation went on every day. I kept asking for hints about this "biggest star in the world," but he held firm, no hints.

"You *have* no comedy project," I challenged, "and no 'biggest star in the world.' You've been practical joking me, haven't you?"

"Make a deal," he said, extending his hand, "and see if I'm practically joking you."

This silly game went on until, at a dinner party at the home of the renowned fashion designer Oscar de la Renta, I forced Mr. Bluhdorn to divulge the name of the world's biggest star. I was seated to the left of the flamboyant editor of *Vogue,* Diane Vreeland, who found me utterly fascinating. She told me this many times after commandeering my right arm and keeping me from eating a succulent-looking veal chop. During that spell when Ms. Vreeland clutched my wrist in a viselike grip, I challenged Mr. Bluhdorn to play a version of twenty questions with me.

"I'll give you a hundred," he said chivalrously.

"I won't need a hundred, but if I guess that star's name," I asked, "will you tell me?"

"No, RRRReiner." He chuckled, devilishly. "I will *not* tell you, but I will give you a thumbs-up."

For the next half hour, while enjoying my dessert and coffee, we played. Ms. Vreeland set my arm free during the salad course. When we began, I was confident I'd guess because there were fewer than twenty actors in the world who are in the biggest-star-in-the-world category. It must be noted that this game took place in 1978, so the stars we mentioned were the reigning ones at that time.

"Barbra Streisand!" I offered.

"*Bigger!*" he countered, grinning wildly.

"Richard Burton!"

"*Bigger!*"

"Elizabeth Taylor!"

"*Bigger!*"

"Bigger than Burton and Taylor??"

"*Bigger! Bigger!*"

"Robert Redford!"

"*Bigger!*"

"Paul Newman!"

"*Bigger!*"

"Sidney Poitier!"

"*Bigger!*"

"Bigger than Streisand, Burton, Taylor, Redford, Newman, and Poitier?" I asked.

"*Bigger!*" he shouted. "*Much bigger!*"

"There are no stars bigger than those!" I insisted.

"There is *one!*"

Mr. Bluhdorn countered with "*Bigger!*" after I, and the amused dinner guests offered the following names:

Julie Andrews, Laurence Olivier, Jimmy Stewart, Bette Davis, Alec Guinness, Paul Scofield, Warren Beatty, Anne Bancroft, Spencer Tracy, Jack Lemmon, Walter Matthau, Shirley Maclaine, Gene Kelly, Frank Sinatra, Sammy Davis Jr., Bob Hope, Al Pacino, Charles Laughton, Charlie Chaplin, Tyrone Power, Greer Garson, Danny Kaye, Peter Sellers, Clark Gable, Jimmy Cagney, Woody Allen, Robert DeNiro, Dustin Hoffman, Paul Muni, and I don't remember how many more. After some of our guesses, we heard, "*HE'S DEAD!*" or "*SHE'S DEAD!*"

He loved this game. The more frustrated we all became, the happier he was. He was drunk with power, and since I was the one empowering him, I decided to sober him up by capitulating.

"I'm sorry, sir, game's over!" I sighed. "I have exhausted my list and everyone's else's list of 'biggest stars.'"

"Well, Mr. RRRReiner," Mr. Bluhdorn snarled, his eyes dancing, "you left off your lists, the . . . one . . . and . . . only *biggest star in the world!*"

"Who?" I asked, sarcastically. "Mickey Mouse?"

"*NO!*" he screamed. "*Fidel Castro!*"

As if we had been rehearsed, all of us responded in unison, "*Fidel Castro???*"

"Hah, RRRReiner, never thought of Castro, did you?"

"Biggest star in the world?" I chided. "I don't believe I've seen any of Fidel's films."

"Films? I never said *film* star, and *that is* the point," he said, grinning from ear to ear. "Because he has never been in a film, every newspaper on the planet is going to have the same headline on their front page: 'Fidel Castro, the President of Cuba, Has Agreed to Co-star in a New *Film* for Paramount *Pictures!*'"

I wanted to say "You've got to be kidding!" but I didn't.

"So, RRRReiner," he said triumphantly, proffering his hand, "are you ready to make a deal now?"

"And what part will he be playing?" I said, going along with the madness.

"Fidel Castro will play Fidel Castro!"

"Good casting," I joked, "but not much of a stretch for him. What is the picture, a sort of documentary?"

"I didn't buy a movie company to make documentaries," he explained in a tone I had not heard before, "no, it will be a comedy, a comedy with heart! *The Bad News Bears Go to Cuba*!"

So that's why he invited me! Finally it all made sense. Two successful *Bad News Bears* pictures, why not shoot for a third?

This time there was no hot sun in my eyes when I listened to Mr. Bluhdorn talk about the film, but there was a big knot in my stomach. It seemed that, at a clandestine midnight meeting in Cuba, Fidel had agreed to play himself in three scenes: playing catch with the Cuban Little Leaguers, giving them a pep talk before the big game, and throwing out the first ball and sitting in the stands watching the World Championship game between Cuba and the United States.

Mr. Bluhdorn talked about why I should do the film, and I countered with why I couldn't.

"I'd never be able to stay on schedule," I said, half-facetiously. "Every picture I've ever done, I have brought in on time and under budget. If El Jefe decides to give one of his marathon seven-hour speeches on a day he's scheduled to work . . . I . . ."

"RRRReiner," he interrupted, "you don't want to shake my hand on this one either, do you?"

"No, sir, I don't," I admitted, "mainly because doing a second sequel of *Bad News Bears* or any picture really doesn't interest me."

Mr. Bluhdorn told me that the very talented Michael Ritchie had written the script and was in the process of reworking the end, which had problems.

"Last night I called him on the phone. 'RRRRitchie,' I pleaded, 'wrrrite me a Stella Dallas ending.' RRRReiner, you understand what I'm talking about!"

"Yeah, you want a tearjerker ending."

"*Bigger!* I want the ushers should have to go down the aisles handing out boxes of Kleenex."

I felt so beholden to Mr. Bluhdorn for being so hospitable to us and for being so endearingly whacko that I offered to meet with Michael Ritchie and kick around some ideas, for free, of course.

I spent a couple of very pleasant hours with Michael Ritchie, comparing notes about our eccentric billionaire benefactor and also attempting to find a nonmanipulative, sentimental ending. Ritchie admitted he had no heart for the piece but got roped into it by falling for the shake-my-hand-and-you-got-a-deal ploy. Michael had considered an ending in which the coaches and umpires decide that, after playing thirty innings, with the scored tied at 0–0, both teams are winners and order that they share the trophy, each team holding it for six months a year. After coming up with a few more dopey and overly sentimental ideas, we got giddy enough to take a shot at Bluhdorn's Kleenex-box-with-no-dry-eye-in-the-house ending. We came up with the following shot list:

Close-up of

- the coaches and players on both teams fighting back tears.
- the kids' parents, grandparents, and relatives dabbing at their eyes.
- millions of misty-eyed baseball fans blinking and smiling.
- Little Leaguers in uniform watching the World Series on TV and wiping their drippy noses on their sleeves.
- Presidents Nixon and Castro fighting back tears and losing that fight.
- tears of joy rolling down the two president's cheeks.
- the closing credits start rolling and the tears of joy that were rolling down the presidential cheeks splash all over the closing credits and roll into the orchestra pit.

As I am sure you are all aware, *The Bad News Bears Go to Cuba* was never made, and I believe that is why, to this day, Fidel Castro is so pissed off at the United States.

21

The Emergency Gourmet Dinner

In the late '50s and early '60s, a group of talented authors, writers, artists, performers, and businessmen got together and formed the Gourmet Eating Club. The club would meet at least two or three times a month to dine at a Chinese restaurant in New York's Chinatown. Ngoot Lee, a Chinese food maven and a serious painter, who was born in China, and lived in Chinatown, was charged with the responsibility of choosing the best restaurants for their gourmet eating meetings. He chose a restaurant not for its decor but for the culinary excellence of its chef. I had heard about this extraordinary gourmet eating club from Mel Brooks and Joe Stein, two of an eclectic group, which included novelists Mario Puzo, Joe Heller, and George Mandel; actor Zero Mostel; businessman Speed Vogel; and diamond merchant Juley Green. All shared a need to laugh, eat gourmet Chinese food, and get out of the house for a night with the boys.

While living and working in Los Angeles, I made many quick trips to New York and longed to be a part of that gourmet dining experience. Joe Stein had proposed my name to the club members and recommend that I be invited as a guest eater. I was told that, after serious and spirited deliberation, the members voted that I be a permitted to join them for one of their gourmet dinners—but only for one! A second invitation was possible and would depend upon my social behavior and my willingness to chip in for the food.

As bad luck would have it, the days I spent in New York were always days when the club was not scheduled to meet. Consequently, I never had the pleasure of accepting their semigracious invitation. On the day of my fourth unsuccessful attempt to join them, I was preparing to fly home frustrated and unfulfilled, when Joe Stein called.

"Carl," Joe said excitedly, "good news! The club voted to convene an emergency Chinese dinner tonight, just for you! That is, if you're available—if you're not, we'll convene without you."

Because of the short notice, only Joe Heller, Joe Stein, George Mandel, Speed Vogel, Mel Brooks, and Juley Green, were able to convince their wives that it was imperative they leave their homes to attend an emergency gourmet dinner they had arranged for a needy friend. Ngoot Lee asked that we rendezvous in Chinatown at a designated street corner from whence he would lead us to a new restaurant.

Joe Stein, our self-designated driver, chauffeured Joe Heller, Mel Brooks, and me to Chinatown, where we found Ngoot and the other club members waiting at the designated corner. Joe Heller, the hungriest member of the club and its most dedicated eater, jumped out of the car and confronted Ngoot.

"This new restaurant," Joe Heller challenged, "is it as good as our old one?"

"*New* one is good as *old* one," Ngoot said, with his textbook Chinese accent, "I guarantee!"

"How do you know?" Joe Heller challenged.

"I know because *new* one steal chef from *old* one!"

"Good enough! Take us to your restaurant!"

"I take you," Ngoot said, "in one minute!"

With that, Ngoot dashed across the street toward an apartment building.

Where the hell are you going? we all thought, but Joe Heller shouted it.

"I go visit wife and say hi!" Ngoot yelled back and ran into the building.

I was told then that Ngoot had befriended a young Chinese immigrant whose visa had expired. To keep her from being deported, he married her and set her up in a one-room, fifth-floor apartment. Before Joe Heller could finish grousing about Ngoot's dinner-delaying detour, Ngoot came bounding out of the building and back across the street.

"Wasn't she home?" one of us asked.

"She home," Ngoot answered, puffing hard.

"Didn't have much time to say hi to your wife, did you?" Joe offered.

"Enough. I open door, visit, say 'Hi, wife!' close door, and go."

Ngoot's lightning visit served two purposes, he showed his wife he cared, and he made his friends laugh. Ngoot and his wife had started their marriage living apart, and he visited her only when it pleased him. As time went on Ngoot and his wife bonded and he invited her to move in with him. He had fallen in love with her, and told the group about the serious commitment and gift he made to her. He described, in detail, how, on one sunny afternoon, he put his arm around her waist and escorted her to the kitchen window, where on the sill was an herb garden growing in a two-foot-long window box.

"Someday, sweetheart," Ngoot said solemnly, his hand sweeping majestically across the small window box, "this land aaaaall gonna be yours!"

Since then, I never pass a flower-filled window box without saying, "Someday, aaaall this land gonna be yours!"

Ngoot seated us at a round table in the rather small, unprepossessing new restaurant. From my seat, I had a clear view of the kitchen and the activity that went on in it. I had just settled in my chair when Ngoot jumped up and said that he thought I might be more comfortable sitting in his seat. I was perfectly comfortable where I was, but Ngoot insisted that, since I was the honored guest, I sit with my back to the kitchen instead of facing it. I thought it strange, and I asked if this was some kind of Chinese tradition.

"Traditionally," Joe Heller explained, "honored guests, who aren't accustomed to seeing a rat scurry across a kitchen floor, don't seem to enjoy the evening as much as those of us who are accustomed to the intrusion."

I thought Heller was kidding but two others confirmed seeing "the little feller" scurrying about.

No one seemed upset about the "visitor," and all had a creative reason for not leaving. For example:

"All New York restaurants have problems with vermin."

"Yeah, but the ritzy ones hide them by keeping their kitchen doors closed."

"Which is dishonest! This is an honest restaurant with an open-door policy!"

"Right, so we stay?"

"We have to. At this hour no good, rat-free restaurant is still open."

"I'm starved!"

The ordering was, by and large, left to Ngoot, with major input from Heller and, for aesthetic and allergy concerns, special needs ordering by Brooks and Stein. The rest of us opted to wait and taste. My memory of things said and eaten that night might be a little fuzzy, but the following is clear.

The first course was an impressive-looking special winter melon soup. An immense scooped-out winter melon, which served as its own soup tureen, was placed on the table. As soon as the waiter took off the top of the melon, Joe Heller stood up and grabbed the ladle.

"This is a special night," he announced, smiling at me, "and in honor of our special guest, *I* will serve!"

He filled one of the bowls with the piping hot soup, handed me the ladle and, said, "Now *you* serve!"

It was obviously one of the club's rituals that Heller had designed to ensure that he got his fair share of soup in case there weren't enough fair shares to go around. Heller, to help me avoid breaching any of the club's rules, informed me of the one rule that is strictly enforced. The "touch-rice" rule, which Heller himself had drafted.

The touch-rice rule made it illegal to put your chopsticks into one of the communal serving platters and pick up a piece of the succulent lobster, duck, pork, beef, or shrimp without first "touching rice," i.e., putting some of the inexpensive white rice into your mouth between each chunk of the expensive stuff.

Heller insisted that the touch-rice rule was necessary to stop the more piggish gourmets from turning into gourmands, but most agreed that its main function was to ensure that nobody in the club ate more than Joe Heller. Even though Heller invented the the touch-rice rule and strictly enforced it, he rarely obeyed it. Being a former army air force captain, he firmly believed that "rank has its privileges."

I considered the evening a great success. The food was exceptional, the laughs were many, and as far as I knew, sitting with my back to the kitchen, the "little feller" did not appear again.

Aside from being invited to eat with the club again, the thing about that evening that stays alive in my memory is the request Joe Heller made to Joe Stein on our ride back home. As most literate people in the world are aware, Joe Heller was the author of *Catch 22,* the most talked-about and praised book of the era, now considered a classic. He had also written a play, *We Bombed in New Haven*, which had opened on Broadway a few nights earlier. It had been fairly well received but not nearly as well as his novel.

"Hey, Joe," Heller asked Joe Stein, who was at the wheel, "how are you planning to drop us off?"

"Well," Stein answered, "I'll drop Carl at the Sherry Netherlands, continue uptown, drop Mel, then cut across the park and drop you. Why?"

"Before you drop anybody, could we swing by my theater?" Heller asked, simply, "I'd like to stop by for a few minutes."

"Hey, Joe, it's one A.M.! If you're looking to hear some reaction," Mel Brooks offered, "the audience has dispersed, and you can't trust the reaction of a dispersed audience. Let's go home!"

Joe Heller, if he is anything, is persuasive. Without telling us why he wanted to swing by the theater, he prevailed, and there we were approaching the Golden Theater on West Forty-fifth Street. Joe Heller directed Joe Stein to stop the car about thirty feet before getting to the theater entrance and to park on the other side of the street.

"Now what?" Joe Stein asked.

"Now," Joe Heller replied, rolling down his window, "I sit and look at the marquee."

On the marquee, in lights, or I should say, in bulbs, as the electricity had been turned off, was: *They Bombed in New Haven,* A New Play by Joseph Heller. We all sat silently for a few minutes and looked at Joe Heller looking at the sign. He didn't speak for a long time. He didn't have to. Being in show business, we knew why he wanted to swing by the theater. When he did speak, he articulated it for all of us.

"Just wanted to see my name up there. I never thought I'd be on a Broadway theater marquee, and there I am! It's very exciting! Don't know how long the play will run or if I'll ever write another one so, if you guys don't mind—a couple more minutes?"

We sat for a few more minutes before Heller said, "Okay, Joe, drive!"

I met with Joe Heller a few times over the course of the years and could never reconcile the sentimental Joe Heller who stared silently at his name on the theater marquee and the me-first gourmand Joe Heller who created the touch-rice rule. Obviously, he reconciled them well enough to have created an impressive body of literary work and a tremendous capacity for making and keeping good friends and an even bigger capacity for ingesting enormous amounts of gourmet Chinese food without ever saying, "I think I ate too much."

22

Honoring Renoir and Embarrassing Others

For no good reason but to amuse myself, I have decided to tell this true story in the form of a play.

CAST
(as themselves)
in almost alphabetical order:

Barbara Bain . . . . literate blond actress

Martin Landau . . . . . . wide-mouthed distinguished actor

Jeffrey Hayden . . . . . . smiling dinner guest/film director

Jean Renoir . . . . beloved honored guest/film director

Dido Renoir . . . . beloved wife of beloved guest

Estelle Reiner . . . . hostess par excellence/jazz singer

Carl Reiner . . . . hostess' helper/author

Aaron Ruben . . . . short reconteur/writer-producer

Sandy Ruben . . . . excellent conversationalist/personal
                                                 manager

Connie Russell . . . . . . excellent vocalist/wife/mother

Eva Marie Saint . . . . . former high school cheerleader/
actress

Mike Zimring . . . . most civilized of all Hollywood
agents

Act One, Scene One: Mike Zimring's office of
the William Morris Agency. Carl Reiner and
his agent, Mike, are discussing another of
Mike's clients.

CARL

Mike, I gotta thank you. In my wildest
dreams I never thought I'd actually meet Jean
Renoir, let alone be invited to his house for
dinner. And he seemed to like my movie
(*Enter Laughing*). By the way, I appreciate your
suggesting it.

MIKE

I didn't, he asked to see it.

CARL

I know you set it up, and I'm glad you did.
What a night! Estelle and I haven't stopped
talking about the man. He's so lovable.

MIKE

I warned you, to meet him is to fall in love
with him. That's one of the reasons I hate
introducing him to my friends. He's getting on
in years and can't socialize as much as we
would like him to. It's frustrating.

CARL

Mike, Estelle and I were talking. Dido really
put herself out making that great meal, and
we'd like to reciprocate. Do you think she and

Jean would come to dinner at our house? My
friends are dying to meet Renoir. Could you
ask him?

MIKE

Hey, Carl, I handle Jean Renoir for films, not
for dinner parties. Call him. I bet he'd love to
come.

Scene Two: *the* Reiner *home.*
Later that day.
[Carl *enters house,* Estelle *meets him in foyer*]
CARL
[*Taking off jacket*]

So?

ESTELLE

I called everybody, and half of them had
something planned for that night.

CARL

Damn. How many are coming?

ESTELLE

Everybody! They changed their plans when I
told them we're serving tête de veau and that
Jean Renoir would be here, and after dinner
we would screen *La Grande Illusion.*

What I am trying to establish in these first two scenes is that
Jean Renoir was a much-loved man, that we were planning to
serve calf's head vinaigrette for dinner, and screen his classic
film after it. I thought I did it fairly well, but seeing how much
paper I used to give you so little information, I conclude that
my effort to playwrite this story is not cost efficient.

All of the guests who were on my cast list did show up and

were as thrilled as we were to be a part of what turned out to be the most memorable of all the memorable dinners that we had ever given. Estelle felt, as I do, that guests really appreciate it when you exert that extra effort to present a meal that is not only delicious but rarely served in a home. What better choice for a dinner honoring our French film legend than the classic tête de veau, an elegantly prepared peasant dish about which we have been raving since eating it at the elegant Lucas Carton, a two-star Parisian restaurant. We went blithely about preparing to produce this exotic meal, unaware that there was not a calf's head to be found in all of Beverly Hills nor its neighboring towns. After dozens of attempts we finally located not a calf's head but a cow's head. So committed were we to serving this meal that we went forward and Estelle managed to deliver a darn good facsimile of the original. If we are to believe our guest of honor, and who would question a man who sports a Légion d'honneur on his lapel, our tête de cow was *"better than,"* or he might have said, *"bigger than,"* any he had ever eaten. Jean Renoir's French accent was rather thick and I might have misunderstood him; however, there was no doubt that the dish was a hit.

You may think that I am lingering too long on what we served but the night's menu plays a key role in this tale. To complement our pièce de résistance, Estelle served a side dish she had created which received kudos, and, more importantly, requests for second helpings. Lucas Carton would kill to get his hands on Estelle's recipe for sauteed cabbage in Champagne–sour cream sauce.

Earlier that day Mike Zimring called me to say that Dido was concerned about Jean's stamina.

"You know," Mike said, "Jean is getting on in years and has

difficulty staying up too late. He is usually in bed by ten, so unless we can eat dinner pretty early, the old gent might not make it through his movie."

So excited was everyone to see *La Grande Illusion* and hear the great filmmaker discuss the making of his masterpiece that all were in their seats and ready to eat at six o'clock sharp—even one chronically late friend, whom I would single out if I thought he were curable.

When I say that we screened the film in our den, I don't want to give the impression that we had an elaborate screening room in our home. I had a window-shade-type pull-down screen onto which I projected Jean Renoir's personal print on the sixteen-millimeter projector I received as a gift for my appearance on *This Is Your Life*.

Before I started the projector I thanked M. Renoir, who insisted we call him Jean, and told him how fortunate we all felt that he had lent us both his presence and his print of *La Grande Illusion* for the screening. He said that he felt fortunate there was a print to lend. He had not owned or seen the film since the war. Adolf Hitler found this masterwork, this brilliant treatise on the madness of war and of the people who perpetuate war, to be dangerous and inflammatory anti-Nazi propaganda. He had ordered all prints of *La Grande Illusion* to be torched. The Gestapo were successful conquering all of Europe and burning every print that existed. By the end of the war, only a few terribly abridged versions of the film existed, lovingly spliced together from snips and clips by editors who knew the value of this work of film art.

Jean Renoir told us that a year or so earlier he had received a call from a man in Paris who said that he was cleaning out a cellar and found a big metal container full of funny flat cans that had the name Jean Renoir written on them. The cans contained a kind of bluish-looking film.

"It looks like some kind of spoiled film," the man guessed, and wanted to know if Renoir had any interest in looking at them before he tossed them out. Renoir knew immediately that this was the original negative of the film Hitler had thought he destroyed. What Jean didn't know was that the negative was in pristine condition.

"So," Renoir joked, "you never know what you're going to find in the trash."

After the viewing, all of us had the same reaction: the film had lost none of its beauty and power. For the next two or three hours, M. Renoir told us wonderfully personal stories about each member of the cast. I was surprised to learn that the star of the film, Jean Gabin, had no experience as an actor before Renoir cast him. I was also happy to watch Erich von Stroheim again being the philosophic German officer. In my career I have impersonated Herr von Stroheim many times, General von Cluck in *Dead Men Don't Wear Plaid* being my last and most successful thievery.

The most wonderful and terrible part of the evening was that it lasted until one o'clock in the morning. Wonderful that all of us had, as Mike Zimring prophesied, fallen deeply in love with this utterly irresistible old man. Wonderful that Estelle and I had hosted a party at which our guest of honor felt comfortable enough to stay three hours past his curfew. But terrible that an evening that went so smashingly could turn sour in the flush of a toilet. It happened at exactly 12:40 A.M. Yes, Detective, I can be sure of the time, because out of concern for M. Renoir's comfort, I kept checking my watch. It seemed no one wanted the evening to end.

It was at precisely 12:40 A.M. that I detected a smell coming from the powder room, which is located less than ten feet from the bar, where all our guests were gathered. Three or four or more of our guest had made use of the powder room in those last eventful minutes, the last being the prime suspect, a beautiful blond who, in every Raymond Chandler–type novel would be the last to be suspected. But I was a more than credible eyewitness who would swear that the awful smell emanating from the powder room was not present before the three-time Emmy Award–winning actress, Barbara Bain, had gone into it. I will testify under oath to hearing the flush moments before smelling the smell. Estelle and I traded glances and grimaced, with a what-the-hell-is-that? expression on our faces. Barbara Bain came blithely out of the powder room and smilingly rejoined the crowd. No one seemed to smell what my wife and I were smelling, or if they did they were acting as though they didn't, which, with this group, was possible, considering that Eva Marie Saint and later in his career, Martin Landau received Oscars for acting. Estelle and I, with small eye and head signals, left to confer in the kitchen.

"Oh, my God," one of us said.

"It's gotta be the cabbage dish," I think I said.

"It's never had that effect on anybody before," I think she said.

"Did you put anything different in it?" I know I asked.

"What do we do?" she said.

"Get Renoir out of the house," I said, "at his age these fumes could be lethal!"

We went back into the den only to find that Sandy Ruben was missing. To our shock, she had dared to use the powder room. The stench was worse than ever, and she, like Barbara Bain, came out of the gas chamber smiling. I suddenly remembered that a few minutes earlier the other beautiful blond, Eva Marie Saint, had preceded Barbara into the powder room. I began to wonder if I was in danger of fingering the wrong blond. Then I thought, there is no chance that this is the work of one of our lovely, delicate women. It had to be one of the men. While these thoughts ran through my head, I did all the things polite hosts do to hint to their guests that the evening is over. It literally took another ten or fifteen minutes to herd all the suspects out the front door. Yes, I considered them all suspects. No one person could have created such a pungent bomb.

After the good-byes at the door, and as far as I was concerned they were perfunctory, because all I could think about was finding the source of the offensive odor, and wondering why no one but my wife and I seemed to be aware of it. I sniffed my way from the powder room to the bar and found that the odor was becoming increasingly bad as I made my way to the little pantry that abuts the bar. I considered that it might be a broken pipe that flowed from the powder room and the bar and pantry area. At two in the morning I traced it to the crawl space under the house. I could hardly wait for morning, when I could call some foul-smell expert to find and repair what needed to be repaired. A plumber, along with someone from the health department, diagnosed our problem. Three factors came into play that almost ruined our wonderful evening. If these factors had converged during dinner or at the screening, I would not be writing this anecdote—or maybe I would, but it couldn't have as happy an ending.

The three factors:

1. One of the small mesh-covered vents in the foundation that allow air to flow under the house was ajar.

2. A stray cat had, weeks or months earlier, squeezed itself through the small opening and had not been able to find its way out.

3. A Santa Ana wind kicked up and, without a permit, blew through Beverly Hills. A particularly strong gust had whooshed through the crawl space under our house, wafting the aroma of putrefying cat up through the basement and into our house.

A gas-masked city worker, wearing heavy work gloves and carrying a very long pole with tongs at the end, removed the poor animal, fumigated the area, and earned our undying respect and admiration.

The following morning each of our guests received this letter:

The morning after

Dear _____

It was neither the woman to your right nor the man to your left nor Estelle's Champagne, cabbage, and sour cream dish, nor her magnificent tête de vache nor anything to do with the powder room or its users, it had to do with a poor benighted, putrefying cat who had lost its way under our house. Its presence may have never been known had not a powerful Santa Ana wind blown in from the desert and under our home at 12:45 A.M. this day. I hope you didn't, as I did, falsely accuse Barbara Bain for fouling our lovely atmosphere. The woman has been completely exonerated.

     Fondly,
     Carl

For the next day or two we received calls and notes from all the "suspects," who admitted that they had all thought as I did, and were relieved to discover the truth. What a great and talented group of dissemblers! They would not, for one moment, let on that the glorious evening we shared, honoring Jean Renoir, stank to high heavens.

23

Perpetual Papa

Lenny Grotte and I were seven or eight years old when we had this discussion about the First World War, which had ended about ten years earlier.

"We won the war," my friend Lenny insisted, "because we had lots more big boats with big cannons and guns and bullets and airoplanes with machine guns and bombs and we had a gigantiker army with a zillion soldiers with rifles and bayonests!"

"My papa wouldn't need no zillion soldiers with rifles," I boasted, "he coulda won the war by using straggedy."

I didn't know exactly what "straggedy" was, but I knew that my father knew, because he knew everything and had told me many times that there was always a better way to do something if you used your brains and found the right "straggedy."

I had great respect for my father and never doubted that whatever he told me was true. Since then I have learned that you can't win anything with "straggedy," but a proper use of strategy can, at times, help to win baseball games, elections, and a tic-tac-toe match.

When I was small, I thought Papa was tall. He was a couple of inches taller than his two brothers, Harry and Max. At five foot four, Papa was the tallest one in our family; my mother was five foot two and my brother, at age eight, was at least a head shorter than our parents. Papa always walked tall, holding his head high and his shoulders squared. When my brother and I grew to be six feet and six two respectively, I asked Pa how we got to be so tall.

"You take after your grandfather. He was tall," he said proudly, "almost five foot six!"

He attributed some of our growth to the daily tablespoonful of cod liver oil he insisted we take.

In 1900, at age fourteen, my father, Irving Reiner, né Usher Reiner, left his home in Czernowitz, Romania, and traveled to Vienna to accept a position at a large jewelry store as a master watchmaker. In those days, to be certified as a master watchmaker, one had to be able to make all the parts of the watch except the mainspring. My father, his four brothers, my grandfather, my great-grandfather, and for generations back, we're not sure how many, were all watchmakers. My father, hoping that my brother, Charlie, and I would find careers that would not tie us to a workbench, chose not to teach us how to repair watches.

To define my father simply as a watchmaker is not giving him his due. In these next pages I would like to give him that.

I always knew my father was special because he did so many things that my friends' fathers didn't do. Here is a partial list of some of those things.

My pop was a self-taught violinist and flautist. In 1906, when Pop was twenty, he emigrated to America, found a job in Union City, New Jersey, bought a Bohemian-crafted violin for the princely sum of $500, an ebony flute, two how-to books of instructions, and proceeded to teach himself to play both instruments and how to read and transpose music. After auditioning for the Leo Prinz Symphony Orchestra, my best memory of the amateur forty-piece orchestra's name, he was invited to play second violin and/or first flute at the free weekend concerts that the orchestra gave in public parks, libraries, and prisons.

He did all of his concertizing before he married my mom, and for one year after my brother, Charlie, arrived. I remember fondly the stacks of music portfolios sitting in the corner of the bedroom and his playing me to sleep with sweet-sounding flute solos, and his always obliging me when I asked for "one more, just one more!"

But mostly I remember my pop inventing things—a lot of things. Among his inventions were:

1. a timing attachment for a camera that allowed the photographer to step into the family picture he was snapping (1913) (a Japanese inventor patented a similar device six months before my father applied. I still have Pop's prototype timer);
2. a self-winding wristwatch (1927–28);
3. an automobile clock (patented 1930);
4. an electric clock, powered by a flashlight battery (patented 1930);
5. a high-voltage, low-amperage battery to power a clock for a hundred years without being changed or recharged (1930–53, patented 1953);
6. a clock powered by the above quasi-perpetual battery (1930–1953, patented 1953).

THE GENESIS OF THE CLOCK THAT INSPIRED THE CHAPTER TITLE "PERPETUAL PAPA"

"What are you doing, Papa?" is something I often asked. I remember coming home from school one day and seeing him quickly toss something into one of the drawers of his workbench. From the time I was six until he retired, he worked at home. I asked him what he was working on, and he said he couldn't tell me.

"Why can't you tell me, Papa?"

"*Seig nicht ein nahr halb arbeit!*" he answered.

"What does that mean?"

"It is an old German-Jewish saying," he said, smiling. "It means, 'Don't show a fool half work.'"

He explained that "fool" in this sense meant one who could not appreciate or understand what the end product might be.

My father worked on his inventions on Saturday and Sunday nights, when the family slept. One Sunday, I wandered into the kitchen and caught him sitting at the kitchen table on which were lying dozens and dozens of round pieces of white paper. With a small jeweler's file in one hand, a sheet of white paper in the other, under which he held a dime-sized tempered-steel disk, he rubbed the rasp against the paper-covered steel disk and produced a dime-sized piece of paper. Using his jeweler's loupe, he would examine each paper circle and check it for burrs or imperfections—the imperfect ones he would discard. Had he been able to afford a punch press, the two thousand disks that it took a year to make by hand could have been extruded by a machine in minutes.

I had caught him in the act of inventing, and for some reason he allowed me to watch him work. Was I ever fascinated! When the table was filled with the little pieces of round paper, he would pick up each one with a fine tweezer and, with a small brush, carefully paint one side of the paper with a black, inky fluid. He would then hold the paper disk between his thumb and forefinger and paint the tiny bald spot where the tweezer had held it, and then gingerly lay it on the table to dry. This process would continue until all the paper disks were coated and dried. Before making and painting a new batch, he collected the painted disks, arranged them into a small pile, painted side down, and carefully slid them into a foot-long black tube. The process took a year of Sundays and I was there when he finished packing the second of the two tubes.

What he had built was a dry-pile static-electricity battery that he hoped would power a pendulum clock. I remember him taking a piece of cotton thread, making a little knot at the end of it, and then letting the knot hang between the two paper-filled tubes that stood upright about three inches apart. He expected that the knot would be attracted to one of the tubes, pick up a positive charge generated by one of the dry piles, be repelled by it, and then be attracted to the other tube that was negatively charged, pick up that opposing charge, be repelled by it, etc., etc., etc. He foresaw that this attracting and repelling process might well continue for a hundred years. His plan was to build a clock with a simple escapement for the hands and have a pendulum swing between the two static-electricity batteries to generate enough power to move the hands. And this time it worked! I say "this time" because a year before, he had built two dry piles using the wrong paper and the wrong chemical coating for the two thousand other paper disks that failed to attract the cotton knot.

On this second attempt he used a more porous paper and coated it with magnesium compound instead of a silver one.

He continued to work on this project for many years, finally handcrafting a handsome brass-trimmed, glass-domed pendulum clock. He was awarded two patents, one for the simple three-geared clock and one for a static-electricity battery that was capable of delivering two thousand volts and one milliamp.

By the time the patent papers came through, the clock had been in our dining/living room, proudly perched atop a breakfront—or china closet, as my folks referred to it—and had been ticking away for more than twenty years without once stopping. It was 1953, and I was in my third year of working with Sid Caesar on *Your Show of Shows,* which, that year, was being sponsored by the Bulova Watch Company.

At an after-show dinner party, one of the company's representatives lent me his ear, into which I poured some of the details of my father's perpetual-motion clock. He was both interested and skeptical, and invited me, my father, and his clock to visit the corporate offices that coming week.

While waiting in the reception area of the Bulova Watch Company's impressive offices, a handsome Saville Row–suited man sporting a deep tan and slicked-back graying hair came in, introduced himself as Arde Bulova, shook our hands, and good-naturedly warned my father that his chief engineer had voiced skepticism about what we had claimed for the clock, and then he breezed out.

The skeptical engineer's assistant, who was, no doubt, equally skeptical, invited us into an office and said that the chief engineer would be with us presently. After so many years of work, my pop was about to show his baby to someone who had the means to manufacture it. I was nervous for him but he was his cool scientific self. The chief engineer, wearing a white lab coat, entered, shook our hands, and got right down to business.

"To be perfectly honest with you, Mr. Reiner," he said, addressing my father, "we have doubts that your clock will do what your son says it will, but I am curious. Let's have a look!"

Pop said that he wasn't surprised they were dubious, and went on to explain in great detail everything that went into the making of the clock and his reason for claiming its unusual longevity, citing the fact that in twenty years, the battery tests showed no discernible diminishing of power. They listened attentively, asked a few questions, and after peering at the clock from all angles, the senior engineer said something we had not expected.

"I'll be a son of a bitch! The damn thing works!" he shouted, clapping his hands. "You say this same battery has been powering the clock for twenty years?"

"Over twenty." My father smiled. "I don't have a spare, and I don't intend to build one."

The engineer repeated, "Son of a bitch! That is one helluva clock, Mr. Reiner, one helluva clock!"

He asked my father to leave a copy of the patent papers and promised to get back to us in a few days. When he did, he reiterated how wonderful he thought my father's invention was, but added that it came under the category of a "novelty item rather than an accurate timepiece," and therefore Bulova had no interest in manufacturing it.

My father did not seem to be too upset when I told him their decision, in fact he bolstered their arguments by saying that "pendulum clocks are notoriously inaccurate."

"They must rest on a level surface," he explained, "whether it be on a floor, like a grandfather clock, or a mantle clock like mine, and even if they're leveled off correctly, they have to be reset every week or so."

My father was a true stoic. He had to be terribly disappointed but he showed no signs of being hurt or angry at the rejection.

He and I tried to market the clock one more time. We were invited to appear on a Philadelphia television show called *The Big Idea* where inventors were given the opportunity to do a show-and-tell demonstration of their invention and perhaps pique the interest of some viewing entrepreneur who might deem it worthy of developing.

The afternoon we went in front of the cameras, my years of television experience were of no help. I trembled as I introduced my father to the show's host and the audience. Papa was calm and composed and acquitted himself nobly. Without a bead of sweat on his brow, my Papa the watchmaker became my Papa the science professor. He described, in both technical and layman's language, how the clock was made and what made it tick.

We waited a few weeks. When we did not hear any encouraging words from the show's producers or from their viewers, we knew we had struck out again. My father took the rejection in stride. I think that, like all creative people who would welcome recognition and financial success, he derived enough satisfaction in coming up with a new idea, implementing its development, and seeing it become what he had envisioned it would be.

Earlier, pop had been granted a patent for his clock that was powered by a flashlight battery, which, unlike his perpetual clock, was successfully marketed and made a lot of money—not for Pop but for the company that manufactured it after my father's patent expired. Pop had received the patent right before the depression of the '30s. At that time, most peo-ple opted to spend their money for food, clothing, and shelter rather than for cute battery-operated clocks. During World War II, which followed the Great Depression, cute clocks were not as vital to our nation's survival as big, cute bombers, submarines, and tanks.

Three or four years after the war, the patent on the flashlight-battery clock ran out, and an enterprising German clock company manufactured it. A small victory for our enemy. I like to think that it wasn't a businessman sympa-thetic to the Nazis, but I doubt that back then there were any other kind. Again, my father never showed himself to be bit-ter about this disappointment. To this day, every time I see a clock that runs on a battery, I tell myself or anybody who is with me, "My pop invented that!" My three children, Rob, Annie, Lucas, and my nephew Richie all have a glass-domed battery-driven clock on their mantles—clocks that I bought at a department store and presented to them so that they can remember their grandpa and can tell their children, Jake, Nick, Livia, Romy, Rosie, Rachel, and Max that their "great-grandfather Irving invented that pretty clock on the mantle!"

Pop's perpetual clock outlasted my mother, who passed away in 1963. After her sad passing, I invited my pop to come to Los Angeles to live, which he agreed to do.

My father had packed hastily and took from his Bronx apartment only his clothes, the family photos, his watch-maker's tools, and the dry-pile-battery clock. When he unpacked the clock, which he had hand carried in a little vinyl bag, he shook his head, and said, "Tsk-tsk."

I can remember two other times he was provoked to utter those two discouraging sounds. The first was when I was about fourteen and sitting on the couch reading the sports section while Pa was at his bench repairing a watch. I heard a subtle "tsk-tsk" escape from him. I looked up to see him peering at his index finger. Imbedded in it was the shaft of a jeweler's screwdriver. While tightening a screw, the screwdriver had slipped and gone right through the fleshy part of his finger. Before gingerly unsheathing the screwdriver, he shook his head, and said, "Look what I did—tsk-tsk!"

He delivered another of his low-key tsk-tsks when, at the first test of his perpetual battery, the knotted cotton thread hung limply between the two poles, being neither attracted nor repelled by either battery. After a year's work, his disappointment deserved at least an "Oh, shit!!" or a "Damn, damn, damn!!" But that was my pop. A stoic's stoic with a high threshold for pain.

A third tsk-tsk, which I feel deserves to be catalogued before I return to Pop's perpetual clock, made me look up from the New York Giants box score. It was his reaction to something he was holding in his hand.

"Look at that," he said whimsically, "a silver filling! Do you know how many years that filling has been in my tooth?"

I had no idea.

"Thirty-six years!" he announced proudly.

"How can you remember when that filling was put in?"

"Because," he said, smiling, "I put that filling in myself when I lived in Vienna—lower left molar."

My father went on to explain that he had gone to a dentist to have a couple of cavities taken care of, but the dentist had caused him such pain working on the first tooth that he decided that he would fill the second one himself. Once again, he relied on a book, this time to learn how to fill a tooth. From his dentistry book, he learned how to clean out the decay, sterilize it, and cut the sluices correctly to hold the filling firm, and how to make the proper amalgam of silver and mercury for the filling.

He bought a set of dental tools. Being a watchmaker, he had a hand drill that he used to clean out the decay. He said that because he treated himself gently, he had much less pain than he would have had, had the professional dentist handled the drill. I have yet to meet anyone, dentists included, who has ever filled his own tooth.

Back to the tsk-tsk my father uttered in my California home that provoked those last memories of his stoicism.

"I should have taken a little more care packing the clock." Pop sighed after tsk-tsking loudly. "I shorted the battery! I just wasn't thinking."

He went on to explain that, instead of removing the pendulum, he had left it resting against one of the piles. He had just lost his wife and, as he put it, "my best friend." Who would have expected him to think of anything but that? Bessie and Irving Reiner had been married for forty-seven years and lived in almost perfect symbiosis. Each could do what the other could not do or would not care to do. My father made the rules of discipline, and my mother enforced them, often using a yardstick in the process. For all of their years together, excluding the few months that my father invoked his right to remain silent, sometimes for long periods, it was an eminently successful mating. I think my father considered silence preferable to loud squabbling. It did less harm to the children and kept nosy neighbors out of the loop.

"They don't have to know our business!" was the operative admonition both my parents used when anyone in the family raised his voice.

"Does that mean that the clock won't work?" I asked, concerned that it would not last for the forty more years Pop had conjectured it might.

"We'll see," he said, setting the clock on the fireplace mantle, "it was only shorting for a day."

He gave the pendulum a gentle push, and the clock started up.

"How do you like that." My father smiled. "It still has some juice left."

My father stayed with our family for about five months and got to know his California-born grandson Lucas, who was two and a half, and got to spend time with his older grandchildren, Robbie and Annie. It did my heart good to see them together. My father was a very undemonstrative man, at least that's how I perceived him to be when I was a teenager, but I learned from watching him behave with Lucas and Robbie and Annie, when they were babies, that he was a loving man who kissed and hugged them with fervor. I had to assume that when I was very young, he must have behaved that way with me.

My father returned to New York. After residing at the Hotel Gorham, a rather pleasant apartment hotel on West Fifty-sixth Street in Manhattan, which I had leased for six months, he moved to the Hotel Latham, on Twenty-eighth Street, a "not-so-fancy hotel" where he said he would be "more comfortable." When I visited him there, I understood. It resembled his Bronx apartment in many ways, the most obvious being the age of the building and the crackled porcelain bathroom sink that was an exact duplicate of the one he had washed in at 2089 Arthur Avenue.

I called him often, and we chatted about his grandchildren; my brother and his family; the hotel residents with whom he had become friendly; a lovely old woman, Mrs. Henderson, who he hinted "had eyes" for him.

Pop lived at the Latham for about six years, and never once did we not connect, until the day the switchboard operator informed me that he had checked out and moved to Florida, an absolutely inconceivable move for him to make. He was one of the most hidebound, creatures of habit extant. I called my brother, Charlie, in Cherry Hill, New Jersey, who told me that Pop had awakened with a chest pain and phoned to say that he was not feeling too well. For our pop, who filled his own tooth, to admit to any discomfort sent Charlie speeding to New York to bring him to his home. It was then that we learned what neither of us knew before, that our pop had been suffering with a heart condition for some time, a piece of information that a confirmed stoic would never think to share with anyone, especially his children, and certainly not the hotel operator. Rather than tell her he was moving in with my brother because he was not well, he told her he was going to Florida. My brother assured me that my father, who didn't call me because he didn't want to worry me, was in good spirits. He reassured me that he was fine and happy to be in my brother's home, where he would be able to chat and visit with his teenaged grandchildren, Richie and Elaine.

Estelle and I, on our way to Europe for a two-week summer vacation, stopped off to visit him and were happy to see him up and about and dressed as usual, white shirt, trousers, and vest. Pop had lost a bit of weight and explained that the pills he was taking for his heart and the diuretic pills he took for the edema in his legs had robbed him of his appetite. He said it was a difficult balancing act.

"Well, Pop," I remember saying to him, "you always liked

to experiment with things. Now you can do an experiment on yourself."

"You know something," he said wistfully, "I think that I'll finish that experiment—on the other side."

His exact words.

A week later, while Estelle and I were vacationing in Florence, I received a call from my brother telling me that our father had passed away in the middle of the night. I felt awful that I had not been there for him.

Sharing one of the limos at the funeral, Charlie and I reminisced about our father. We found ourselves laughing at his idiosyncracies and remembering riding with him when we attended our mother's funeral seven years earlier. Pop remarked that one of his oldest friends, Ben Kurtzman, was buried on the other side of the cemetery and wondered if, when he joined my mother, there might be a way to visit him. He considered coming up with some kind of plan for a subway to connect the underground plots. Charlie's wife, Ilse, who was a Holocaust survivor, was understandably upset by our macabre humor and later asked how we could joke about something so sad. I don't really know why we did. It could be that it's a family trait. My father seemed to be comfortable doing that.

The tale of my father's last invention and his passing added another strange coincidence to the two I had described earlier.

Charlie noticed that the perpetual battery, which had been powering Pop's clock for over fifty years, expired—on the very day our father had.

24

An Untitled Memory of Johnny Carson

In the thirty years of Johnny Carson's reign as the host of The Tonight Show, *I was privileged to be his guest forty-seven times. This memory is about one of those appearances.*

Johnny Carson is considered, by everyone who ever owned a television set, to be *the* host of hosts, the greatest ever, and I concur, but to me he is, more importantly, a true and caring friend. It was he who, on February 24, 1981, came into my dressing room twenty minutes before the start of his show and insisted that I cancel my appearance that night and get myself to a hospital.

Earlier that afternoon, about a half hour before I left home, a dull pain had developed in my chest and persisted in making itself felt with every breath I took. I was pretty sure it was a temporary condition, attributable to the large chopped vegetable salad I had eaten for lunch. "Trapped gas" was my wife's diagnosis, and I concurred. She suggested that I would get instant relief by getting into the famous knee-chest position her gynecologist had recommended, and which Estelle had many times used successfully during her three pregnancies. What had worked marvelously for her did nothing for me. The pain was dull and dogged, but remained tolerable enough for me to get into my car and drive to the NBC studios in Burbank.

I had been looking forward to chatting with Johnny about the new film I had directed, which was opening that weekend, and I was determined to go on, pain or no. From the very first time I set foot on a stage, starting when I was seventeen years old, I had never, *ever* missed a performance! Neither snow nor rain nor fever nor flu nor allergies nor dislocated vertebrae nor the skin ripped from my back, could keep me from my appointed performances.*

When I arrived at NBC's famous Studio 2, Johnny Carson, who very quickly became aware of the pain I was experiencing, suggested that I not ignore it and get myself to a hospital emergency ward. He said not to worry about the show, he and Ed McMahon would fill in my time by goofing around a little longer at the top the show. I called my internist, Dr. Norman Bobes, and he agreed with Johnny, but because the pain was tolerable, I was hesitant to leave. I kept thinking, *The show*

-----

*In Hershey, Pennsylvania, the town that smells of chocolate, I had injured my back during a performance of the Broadway bound musical, *Alive and Kicking*, and a local doctor taped it with wide strips of adhesive tape. After five days of performing wearing the corset-sized Band-Aid, I asked Jack Gilford, my dear friend and fellow cast member, to help me remove it. Jack believed that it would be less painful if he yanked the tape off quickly and decisively. I and my raw, skinless back, wept for days, but somehow I managed not to miss one performance.

must go on . . . the show must go on! I struck a compromise with Johnny and the doctor. I would do the ten-minute spot with Johnny, talk about the movie, show a clip from it and thereby keep intact my record of never missing a performance for any reason.

I was the first guest on, and I remember talking very fast, and hearing a lot of laughs. The audience must have sensed that I was in a panic mode, and decided to help out.

Less than an hour after shaking Johnny's hand and waving to the audience, I was lying in a Century City Hospital bed, and being hovered over by Dr. Bobes, whose professional hands were gently pressing on my appendix, gall bladder, and the other places on my abdomen where doctors always press. He ruled out appendicitis, and was almost sure it wasn't my gall bladder giving me the pain, but admitted that he could not make a positive diagnosis until they did a liver scan, which he had ordered for the morning. Since the pain, while still bearable, might worsen during the night, the doctor ordered Demerol, to help me sleep.

The show, which we taped at 5:00 P.M., would be airing that night, and I was curious to see how nutty I had acted, so I eschewed taking the Demerol until after the show. And what do you know—at about midnight, while watching myself on television, and laughing at something Johnny said, I felt the pain in my chest inelegantly and unceremoniously leave my body. The same condition that beset me in Chapter 2, "The Phar-Reaching Phart," resurfaced, but this time, blessedly, there was no Mrs. Mahler staring accusingly at me, and no eight-year-old kids laughing hysterically at the loud, antisocial noise I produced. Now the only laughter heard was my own! I called home immediately, and heard my wife laugh when I told her that her diagnosis had just been proven correct.

Since it is impossible to leave a hospital legally without a doctor's blessings, I had to wait for the morning to be discharged. Morning arrived in my hospital room hours earlier than it did in my home. At 6:30, a compact piece of machinery was wheeled into my room by a smiling, green-clad technician, who woke me up and cheerily announced his intention of doing a scan of my liver. I protested, saying that, as of midnight, I was completely cured, but the smiling technician had his scanning orders, and I owned the liver he was ordered to scan, so, ignoring my wishes, he scanned away. Dr. Bobes arrived an hour later and, after hearing me describe how and why I was feeling so chipper, agreed that the liver scan, which he reported showed my liver to be functioning normally, had not been necessary. He apologized for the inconvenience, and for the zealousness of the gung-ho technician.

About a month after being released, I received an itemized bill for my overnight stay at the hospital. As I checked the bill, I smiled, as I am doing now. Had Johnny Carson not insisted that I rush myself to a hospital, I would have missed the pleasure of end-titling, The Untitled Memory of Johnny Carson, The Twenty-Six-Hundred-Dollar Phart!

25

Lanie Kazan's Box

I have no idea how many benefits I have emceed in my career, but I know that all of them were a success, at least from the standpoint of how I fared as the host. If I had to rate my performances on a scale of one to ten, I would have to brag that all were at least an eight.

"At least an eight?" you ask. "Aren't we being a tad immodest?"

"I don't think so."

"What makes you so cocksure?" I don't blame you for asking.

Well, I could cite the reactions of the audiences, but you might rightly consider that an unverifiable, subjective opinion. I think the irrefutable evidence is the reaction of the Powers That Be who, each year, invite me back. Only one performance, out of the scores that I have done, would I have to rate as a disaster—and sadly, that was a night when I was on my way to a perfect ten.

At this juncture, to make you understand why I seem to be an insufferably pompous ass, I will make you privy to two things: one, a partial list of the black-tie events I have hosted, and two, a personal history of my physical traumas.

BLACK-TIE EVENTS:

Big Brothers Show Biz Bash . . . . twenty-five years
Carl Reiner Tennis Tournament . . . . . twenty-five years
(benefiting the Eras Foundation)
Directors Guild Awards Dinner . . . . . . seventeen years
(and still counting)
Young Musicians Foundation . . . . fifteen years
(and still counting)

HISTORY OF PHYSICAL TRAUMAS:

a sprained arm—1924
a large cinder in right eye that, for removal, required the
trained hand of a neighborhood druggist—1928
badly scraped chin from falling up the stairs (scar still
visible)—1929
six fingertips split open when a firecracker exploded in
hand—1930
right ankle badly gashed by a flying shard of glass—1933
fleshy part of right hand ripped by a rusty backsaw—
1934
two sprained ankles—1934 and 1973
a goodly amount of really nasty paper cuts—1927 to
2003

There you have all the accidents that have befallen me since I stood upright and, except for the paper cuts, they all occurred in the first twelve years of my life. None required heroic measures or even stitches. Not until I hosted the Young Musicians Foundation dinner at the Beverly Hilton Hotel for the tenth time did I ever experience a major trauma. As traumas go, this one was, by far, the most dramatic, inconvenient, painful, and embarrassing one that ever befell me. It is recorded in my memory book as my-longest-recovery-time-from-an-accident-that-could-easily-have-been-avoided-had-somebody-warned-me-of-the-booby-trap.

At this glorious event, young scholarship students sponsored by the Young Musicians Foundation, came from all over the world to perform at the yearly fund-raising event. Young virtuoso soloists are given the opportunity to play and be accompanied by a full-sized symphony orchestra. The orchestra members, led by a budding young conductor, are all under twenty, and if you closed your eyes while they played, you would think you were listening to one of the country's established philharmonic orchestras.

My role was no different than it had been for the dozen or so previous galas. Between introducing the various segments of the show, I look for, and usually find, something to kid about. For the first half of the show, I was doing very well. At these events, to help spur ticket sales, a guest star will graciously lend their presence, and this night it was the wonderful actress-singer Lanie Kazan who would be accompanied by the YMF's youth orchestra.

Most singers, to know how they are blending with their accompaniment, usually employ a monitor. A monitor is nothing more than an unobtrusive black box that houses a small speaker. Unbeknownst to me, while I was at the mike singing her praises in a heartfelt introduction, a stealthy stage-hand quietly placed Lanie Kazan's box on the stage.

I think by now you understand that the title of this anecdote is not a prurient one, although I was aware it sounded like one. Those of you who are not easily offended I think will agree that it was too perfect a title not to use. (I have made my friend Lanie aware of my intentions. She laughed and gave me her blessings.)

The youth orchestra acquitted themselves nobly, and Lanie, as always, was a smash, and the encores the audience demanded were graciously delivered.

Following Lanie Kazan, I was to introduce the fun-filled fund-raising portion of the program that we called the Passing of the Baton. As the auctioneer, I had never failed to extract at least $5,000 from some member of the audience who was thrilled to own a baton that had been passed from the hand of one great Hollywood composer-conductor to the hand of another. Each year, the young musicians were given the opportunity to play the classic themes that would be conducted by the four musical giants who had composed them. Previous years the likes of David Rose, Elmer Bernstein, Pete Rugalo, Jerry Goldsmith, David Raskin, John Williams, and Henry Mancini had participated in the baton-passing ritual. In auctioning off the baton, one of my big selling strategies was pointing out to the bidders how exciting and valuable it would be to own a baton on whose cork handle the sweat of four great conductors had commingled. Every year I would convince someone that dried sweat was even more valuable than moist sweat, and no matter how much they paid for the baton, it would never, ever lose its value—unless they tried to sell it.

I had walked on and off the stage many times that evening. As Lanie Kazan bowed and made her exit stage left, I was standing stage right waiting to make my entrance. In my hand was the baton I would give to Henry Mancini, our first conductor, who was waiting for me to introduce him. I always try to make brisk entrances, as all performers do when they reach a certain age. The older members of the audiences enjoy checking to see if there is still a spring in our step.

I do not remember exactly how many brisk steps I took before I tripped over something that I could not see, and I know had not been there the half dozen times I entered and exited the stage. By now you know that it was Lanie Kazan's box, the black monitor that had been placed on the black stage. With a bright spotlight in my eyes, there was no chance that I could see the perfectly camouflaged black box. My show-offy brisk walk helped propel me high into the air, where, desperately but unsuccessfully, I tried to make purchase with something solid. As I fell to the ground, I remember two things, a quick, sharp pain in my right leg that subsided almost immediately and the audience laughing at what must have looked like my version of Chevy Chase doing his impression of President Ford. I tried to hop up and say something clever, but my right leg just lay there limp and unresponsive to the urgent message my brain was sending it, *Get up, the show must go on!*

At this point, I knew something bad had happened, and I told the audience, very matter-of-factly, "I think something bad just happened," which got a laugh. My wife, who was sitting at a ringside table, did not laugh. She knew, as I did, that I needed really good professional help. I asked for the hand mike, and while lying on my side, put my wife at ease and informed the audience that I was fine and that my pratfall was a real fall. I am not sure, but I think I actually got to say that immortal line, "Is there a doctor in the house?" And there was—an orthopedic surgeon, a Dr. Elconin, who ultimately did the necessary surgical repairs!

My freak accident became the entire focus of the audience's attention, and I knew that there would be no Passing of the Baton until the paramedics carted me off. While lying on the stage chatting with the audience, I saw sitting at a table, and frowning empathetically, one of my oldest and dearest friends, a brilliantly funny man whom I had known in the army and with whom I shared a dressing room when we played in the Broadway musical revue *Inside U.S.A.* Who better to save the day? Before I could finish asking my old buddy Louis Nye if he would come up onstage and take over, he was at the podium and making the audience forget that, five feet to his left, there was a crumpled man waiting for an ambulance. I don't remember what Louis said, but whatever he was saying was getting big, big laughs.

Weeks later somebody who was in the audience said that seeing Louis Nye doing his act while his friend lay prostrate downstage of a group of happy, laughing, fresh-faced violinists, oboists, and timpanists made him feel as if he were in a Fellini movie.

The arrival of the paramedics and the finish of Louis Nye's performance happened simultaneously. Now the entertainment switched to live drama. The audience was totally tuned in to what was happening onstage. I think I got a laugh or two when I balked at a paramedic's decision to free my leg by slitting open my pants with a scissor.

"No!" I screamed. "Not my lucky tuxedo pants!"

Ignoring my protestations they sliced open my pants, straightened my bent leg, splinted it, put me on a stretcher, and carried me off the stage to huge applause and a waiting ambulance.

I was whisked to Cedars-Sinai Hospital where a serious-faced doctor informed me that the tendon in my kneecap (patella) had snapped, causing the long muscle that runs up my thigh, (quadriceps) to "roll up like a window shade." Dr. Elconin and his skilled staff, using a lot of medical and operating-room equipment, snipped off the jagged end of the torn tendon, unrolled my quadriceps, and reattached it to my patella. After doing a magnificent job of suturing the eight-inch incision on my kneecap, (I will display it on request), the doctor assured me that, in a very short time I would be able to walk, trip, and fall as well as ever.

The day following my operation, while recuperating in my room, I received a phone call from a soft-spoken woman who seemed genuinely concerned about my health and well-being. At first I thought it was sweet Edie Rugalo, the chairman of the YMF, and then I assumed that she was a hospital worker or a Grey Lady volunteer. Whoever she was, I assured her that I was being well taken care of and that besides being a little groggy and uncomfortable, I was in no pain. I was happy to chat with someone who seemed to care until I realized that this overly solicitous person was not from the YMF and had not been at the function.

When she asked, "How long do you think this injury will incapacitate you?" and "Do you think you will be able to get back to work pretty soon?" it became clear that I was talking to an insurance company representative. Her next question made me smile. It was a perfect straight line for an old second banana, and I could not resist playing it out until I got that one question I knew must come.

"Mr. Reiner, was there a witness around when you tripped and fell?"

"Oh, yes."

"Do you have that person's name and address?"

"Yes, one was my wife, Estelle Reiner."

"One? Your wife wasn't your only witness?"

"No, there were others."

"How many others?"

"Eleven hundred thirty-six, give or take a few."

I filled in the long pause she took by adding, "That's eleven hundred thirty-six without counting a full symphony orchestra who were behind me when I took the flying leap. I think you should know that all my witnesses, including the orchestra and the conductor, can be trusted to tell the truth—and do you know why?"

"No, why?" was the faint response.

"Because they were all dressed in tuxedos or evening gowns," I answered smugly, "and, as everyone knows, people who dress in formal attire just do not lie."

I assured the flustered woman that I had no intention of suing the hotel or the Young Musicians Foundation or the stagehand who did not remove Lanie's monitor or the paramedic who ripped open my tux pants. I have never sued, or been sued, and I'm proud of that statistic.

With the help of the following: a leg cast; crutches; a cane; my assistant Bess Scher; six months of intensive physical therapy; and my loving wife, Estelle, I regained the use of everything but my tuxedo.

About that ruined tuxedo that I chose to wear that memorable night—I had vacillated between my twelve-hundred-dollar made-to-measure beauty or an emergency backup tux that I bought at C&R Clothiers for $265. If you guessed that I wore my $1,200 job, you'd have guessed wrong. The only pleasure I took from that whole negative experience was knowing that the paramedics were not slicing up the trousers of my expensive tux. I still have that tux and intend to wear it to this year's YMF dinner. If I fall and break anything before this book is published, there will be an addendum to this anecdote.*

---

*I recalled two events I emceed many years earlier which I think a worthy companion to the above piece. On the following pages, you will find "A Recipe to Remember."

26

A Recipe to Remember

Back when the war in Vietnam was raging, many American citizens were raging about the immorality and the indefensibility of the war, and I was one of those citizens. It took me a little longer than some to become aware that what we were doing there was wrong. At the outset, no one wanted to believe we were given false information about the North Vietnamese firing on our ships in the Gulf of Tonkin. The incident, which never happened, precipitated our waging an undeclared war that, thanks to some wrongheaded decisions, caused 58,000 Americans and countless Vietnamese, Cambodians, and Laotians to lose their lives. There are enough words written by American scholars, historians, military men, politicians, and journalists that detail how and why we got into that mess, and I cannot add anything new or revelatory, but I can tell you about the two most emotionally involving appearances I ever made in my career as an emcee.

One of the two anti–Vietnam War events I was asked to host was a New York black-tie fund-raiser in Lincoln Center's Avery Fisher Hall. It boasted an array of stars, that assured a sellout. I had no idea what my opening remarks would be, until I looked at the roster of stars who were scheduled to appear. Barbra Streisand, Paul Newman, Joanne Woodward, Leonard Bernstein, Harry Belafonte, and Sidney Poitier among others. Seeing those names, I immediately thought of the old standard emcee line, "Ladies and gentlemen, I would like to introduce someone who needs no introduction!"

I thought, *A perfect hook for the affair.*

That glittering night, after being introduced and greeted warmly by the formally attired peace-seeking audience, I strode onto the stage of the great hall and announced that I was "a redundancy!"

"Yes, ladies and gentlemen," I insisted, "I am redundant. If ever a show did *not* require the services of a master of cere-monies, this one would be it! There is nothing I can tell you about any one of these great artists that you don't already know. Many of you know these great stars personally, and could probably tell me things about them that I didn't know, or shouldn't know. However, even though I am not needed, I want to be a part of this important event, and to give myself a legitimate function for being onstage, I will, between each star's appearance, give you something that none of these great stars can—a miraculous recipe for cream cheese cook-ies—the world's tastiest, flakiest, and most delicious cookie ever. It was created by Rudolph Stanish, chef to producer Max Liebman, the guiding genius of *Your Show of Shows.* At a private cooking session, Mr. Stanish gave me, my wife, and Nanette Fabray his secret recipe for the cookies—a recipe that I wrote down on a slip of paper, memorized, then ate. Even the paper it was written on was delicious. So grab a pen and jot down this secret recipe for cream cheese cookies. You will thank me."

I was surprised to see some people actually fishing for pens and paper. The first announcement I made, and all that followed, are darned near verbatim.

"A four-ounce package of Philadelphia brand cream cheese—ladies and gentlemen, Mr. Paul Newman!"

Paul Newman, as you might imagine, came onstage to huge applause. I don't remember what he said or did. I was too busy trying to remember a recipe that Estelle and I had made often, but not since we started monitoring our cholesterol intake.

After Paul Newman's appearance, I did not acknowledge how wonderfully he was being received by the audience but simply walked to the microphone, held up my hand, and announced, "A quarter of a pound of sweet butter—Mr. Harry Belafonte!"

As I searched my memory for the next ingredient, Harry Belafonte was doing what he still continues to do, thrill an audience. When he finished thrilling them, I jogged to the mike and with quiet dignity announced, "Nine tablespoons of granulated sugar—Miss Joanne Woodward!"

After a wonderful dramatic reading by Miss Woodward, and an embracing reaction by the audience, I offered, "Nine walnut halves, cut fine—Mr. Sidney Poitier."

For reasons only scholars, who write books on Humor, can explain, the laughter grew heartier each time I announced an ingredient and followed it with a star's name.

By the time I got down to the mixing and baking instructions, the audience was roaring. I started to laugh along with them when I noticed a distinguished gentleman in the first row. It was Joseph S. Clark, a staunch antiwar Senator whom I had met backstage. The audience broke into a sustained applause when I introduced him.

"Senator," I said, laughing, "I am laughing at you because I saw you writing down the cookie recipe . . . and it seemed so mundane a thing for a man of your stature to be doing . . . or was it a new congressional bill you're working on, sir?"

The Senator held up the paper, and called out, "Cream cheese cookie recipe!" His admission provoked many, many hands to shoot up, announcing that they too were jotting down the ingredients.

I think the announcements that provoked the biggest roars were the last two.

"Cream together butter and cheese, add sugar gradually, creaming after each addition, then—add the walnuts—Miss Barbra Streisand!"

And the final one.

"Use a teaspoon to drop a dollop of mixture onto a cookie tin and flatten with—a wet finger!—Maestro Leonard Bernstein!"

Maestro Bernstein accompanied Barbra on the piano, and it was a duo to remember!

After the tremendous applause for their performance died down, I announced, "Bake for ten minutes at three hundred fifty degrees."

In the audience, covering the show for the *New York Post* was Broadway columnist Earl Wilson who, trusting that everything I claimed for the cookies was true, published the cookie recipe in his column. A few day later, my secretary, Sybil Adelman, received a call from Earl Wilson's secretary, who told her about the steady stream of mail her boss was receiving from his readers—disappointed, irate readers. They had all followed the recipe and had no success in making anything that could be described as "the world's greatest cookie."

The world's greatest cookie *disaster* was the tenor of most of the letters.

"They came out terrible," a Texas woman wrote, "I threw them in the garbage!"

"A noncookie!" "A handful of inedible crumbs." "A flaky mess," were the kinds of descriptive phrases Mr. Wilson's readers were motivated to write. They were angry with me for wasting their time and their cream cheese. I sympathized with them. I was a little miffed at Earl Wilson for being sloppy when jotting down my foolproof recipe. I just knew that he had left out an ingredient, and when Sybil reread his column to me, I discovered that he had, indeed, left out a *key* ingredient! A cup of sifted, white flour!

How could he do that? I asked myself.

Easy, I answered, *he's a professional journalist and he—accurately left out the same ingredient that—I left out!"*

Sybil Adelman, who is now a respected comedy writer, immediately contacted Mr. Wilson's secretary, and conveyed my apologies to her boss for my sins of omission.

"If General Motors can recall their cars and trucks," I offered, "I should be allowed to recall my cookies."

The following day, my heartfelt apology was printed in his column, along with the unexpurgated version of Rudolf Stanish's temporarily discredited recipe for cream cheese cookies.

I make no excuses, but I think that one can understand how difficult it was to keep "a cup of sifted white flour" in my head when listening to Streisand sing "People."

Using the newly edited recipe, Sybil baked a batch of the cookies and presented them to me. I found them edible and unexciting, and immediately dictated another note to Earl Wilson, asking him to please tell his readers that when flattening the cookie dough with a wet finger, use a swirling motion starting from the center, and to keep swirling to the outer edge until the dough is wafer thin.

Except for the two cookie recalls, it was a highly successful event, but it took more events, and more raised voices of dissent, before our leaders did the right thing, and declared the undeclared war over.

I mentioned at the outset of this chapter that I was asked to host two of these rallies. Well, for the second one I was made an offer my conscience would not allow me to refuse. The event was called a moratorium, and was to be held at San Francisco's Polo Field on the same day that a similar moratorium was taking place at the Mall in our nation's capital. I should mention that for following my conscience, my name ended up on a list of potential assassins.

The prospect of addressing one million people, the projected attendance, was nerve wracking. I was concerned about putting my physical and professional life in danger. According to the press, the sentiments of the country's entire population were split down the middle, and no performer wants to alienate half his audience. Also crossing my mind was the threat of violence by the crazies to those of us who opposed the war. The murder of students at Kent State University was still fresh in our memory.

Standing on the tallest and widest speakers' platform I had ever been on were the leaders of every citizen's group who opposed the war and wished to be heard. I was awed and proud to have the opportunity to meet Oregon's senator Wayne Morse, who along with Alaska's senator Ernest Gruening were the only members of Congress to vote against the Gulf of Tonkin Resolution. I remember Senator Morse looking out at the mass of humanity, and saying to me, "I have never seen this many people in one place, not even in India."

When I stepped up to the microphone to make my opening remarks, the fleet of helicopters circling the field made it impossible for me to be heard above the sound of the whirring rotors. I asked the sound engineer to crank up the volume on the mike but it didn't help. Neither the news nor the police helicopters seemed to be in any hurry to leave, and if they did not leave, the scheduled speakers would be unable to deliver their messages, and we'd have no rally. After a frustrating few minutes, I shouted into the mike at the top of my lungs, and was able to instruct the crowd by pantomiming that we all look up at the planes and give them the famous victory sign that Winston Churchill used during the Second World War, and to continue the gesture until the pilots got bored and left. It was a sight I will never forget. Hundreds of thousands of faces, all looking to the skies and pumping their V-for-victory sign with both hands. It took a while but it worked. One by one the helicopters peeled off and the rally went on . . . and on . . . and on.

For the next few hours, my co-host, Paul Shrade, an executive in the Electrical Workers Union, and I introduced scores of speakers. Two or three are etched into my memory. Besides Senator Wayne Morse, I remember introducing Reverend Ralph Abernathy, Dr. Martin Luther King's most trusted associate, and a Mr. David Hilliard, president of the Black Panther party.

Mr. Hilliard made a long and impassioned speech that was peppered with words that, even today, only successful rap artists can get away with using in public. He called for the killing of "all those who want to take away your freedom."

"If someone want to take away your freedom," he shouted, "kill the fucker!"

That was the operative phrase that he used over and over, substituting actual names for the word "someone." I was standing next to Rev. Abernathy at that time and I asked him what he thought. He just shook his head, and said, "I have never heard words like that on any podium I ever stood on." Very soon after, David Hilliard, at the top of his voice, bellowed "If Nixon want to take away your freedom, kill the fucker!"

I am certain that I have David Hilliard to thank for my inclusion on President Nixon's assassins list. Whoever compiled the list must have deduced that since I introduced Mr. Hilliard at the rally, I must subscribe to his views on who should be terminated. Until a dear El Paso relative sent it to me, I had not seen the list that was published in a Texas newspaper, but there it was, my name sandwiched between two outspoken critics of the Vietnam War and the most feared, potential assassins in America—Tony Randall and Groucho Marx.

I sighed deeply, then laughed, wouldn't you?

27

Charlie and the President

I could never have guessed that in 1939, a small item in the *New York Daily News* that caught my brother's eye would have the profound impact on my life that it did. Had Charlie not brought it to my attention, I might very well be writing anecdotes about my life as a machinist or, more likely, not be writing anything about anything. What my brother had read was an announcement offering free acting classes to young aspiring actors. The classes were government sponsored, and all that was required was going down to 100 Centre Street in lower Manhattan and applying for admission.

At the time, I was seventeen and gainfully employed as a machinist's helper, delivering millinery sewing machines to ladies' hat factories. My boss, master machinist Abe Weglinsky, had a one-room repair shop that was located at the corner of Thirty-eighth Street and Sixth Avenue, since renamed Avenue of the Americas. Millinery sewing machines were small, but shlepping three of them at a time in bad weather was not as much fun as you would think.

When I was not out delivering, my boss tried to groom me

for a career as a machinist and taught me how to use the lathe to polish needle bars and how to operate a drill press. I was a fair pupil and capable of operating both the lathe and the drill press without hurting myself.

Up until my brother put the *Daily News* clipping in my hand and urged me to apply for the class, I had no thoughts of becoming an actor. Why did he think I did? It could be that my need to do silly walks, make funny faces, belch at will, get laughs retelling jokes I had heard on the radio, and do a perfect impersonation of Ronald Colman in *Lost Horizon* suggested that I harbored a desire to be in show business.

On the first day of the drama class, our teacher, Mrs. Whitmore, a birdlike, white-haired English actress gave us our first assignment. She required everyone in the class to memorize Queen Gertrude's poetic description of the drowning death of Ophelia. I never understood why she thought it important for the male students to learn this speech, but I learned it and it turned out to be a valuable tool for me. To this day, if the occasion arises, and even if it doesn't, I can be counted on to recite it with the same phrasing and dramatic intensity Mrs. Whitmore used when demonstrating how the speech should be delivered.

All the good things that have happened to me in my life I can trace to that two-inch newspaper item my brother handed to me an eon ago—and I acknowledged that from the stage of the Kennedy Center the night I received the Mark Twain Prize. I said then that I owed my show business career to two people: Charlie Reiner, who prodded me to sign up for the free drama class, and Franklin Delano Roosevelt, who established the NRA, the National Recovery Act and the WPA, the Works Projects Administration, the government organizations that financially supported all the lively arts by commissioning works from painters and sculptors and sponsoring programs for the development of dancers, musicians, and, bless him, actors!

That night when I thanked my two benefactors, FDR and my brother, Charlie, had to be one of the proudest and most emotionally gratifying moments of my life. Not only were my wife, all my children and grandchildren, and close and dear members of my family present, but there, sitting among them in the family box, was my brother, Charlie, who had been told four months earlier that he had but a few weeks to live. He had been in a hospice program that was set up in his bedroom, and would have continued with it had not his children, Richard and Elaine, convinced him to try the new cancer drugs that, if effective, would give him more time, time they would appreciate having with him.

He had told me how sorry and disappointed he was that he would not be able to travel to Washington for the October 24 award ceremony. I assured him that he would see the show before the rest of the country. It was not scheduled to be aired until the following February, but I promised to send him a tape as soon as it was edited.

I would call him at his home in Atlanta and get daily updates on his condition from his wife, Ilse, a marvel of a woman, or his caring daughter, my niece, Elaine. The drugs seemed to be working and had helped Charlie to get several weeks past his originally projected expiration date.

A month before the award show, the first in a series of minor miracles started with a call.

"Carl, guess where I am?" he asked playfully.

"In the toilet emptying your catheter bag?" I joked.

It may seem indelicate of me to have made that remark, but those are the things you say when you check in every day for a medical update. There were days of elation when the level of blood in his urine was down, but there were other days when the news was less heartening. On this day, there was excitement in his voice.

"No, I'm not in the toilet!" he answered smugly, "I am in a tuxedo rental store, getting fitted for a tux to wear at that Mark Twain thing—in case I can make it."

And three weeks later, there he was in the family box of the Kennedy Center concert hall, sitting in a wheelchair, wearing his rented in-case-I-can-make-it tuxedo, smiling down at me.

Not only did he "make it" to the event but he "made it" to the party afterward, holding court at a table where, for hours, he chatted, laughed, and shmoozed with what seemed like every member of the audience.

The event was a theatrical highlight for both of us. I appreciated that all of my very good friends and close acquaintances not only showed up but went onstage and said nice things about me and, more importantly, got big, big laughs saying them. One memory that is still very much alive for me was not the event itself but an unexpected aftermath. After the ceremony, I was informed by our producer, Mark Krantz, that the president's appointment secretary had called to invite us to the White House. President Clinton wished to meet and greet our group and present me with the Mark Twain Prize— a photo opportunity I seized and cherished!

The following morning, seated around the large, highly polished table in the meeting room adjacent to the Oval Office were not the president's Cabinet or members of his staff but my grandchildren, Jake, Nick, Livia, and Romy; my wife, Estelle; our children, Rob, Lucas, and Annie; daughters-in-law Michele and Maud; nephews, George Shapiro with his wife, Diane, and Richard Reiner with his wife, Helene, and their children, grand-niece and grand-nephew Rachel and Max; my sister-in-law, Ilse; and Ricardo, a male nurse, who wheeled a smiling Charlie into the room.

Lolling about, in seemingly good spirits, were my dear and giving show biz friends, Dick Van Dyke, Mary Tyler Moore, Steve Martin, Jerry Seinfeld, George Wallace, Richard Belzar, and Joy Behar. Their talent, wit, and gracious presence had, the night before, made the show a roaring success—if we are to trust the audience reaction and the subsequent ratings.

A word about these stars and the tremendous guilt I suffered for allowing the show's producers to intrude on the lives of these busy people by asking them to fly across the continent just to help me receive a prize. It is only because it was the *Mark Twain* Prize that I have managed to exorcize this tremendous guilt.

I thought, as I looked over at Charlie, *This son of a gun beat the odds, or at least improved them enough to be with us on this day.*

When President Clinton arrived, we were all invited into the Oval Office to meet and be photographed with him. He was as charming and gracious as everyone who has ever met him said he was. While the official White House photographer snapped away, the president paused to chat with every one of my family and friends and to hand me the award, a beautifully wrought bronze bust of Mark Twain. I introduced the president to my brother. When I mentioned that Charlie had been in eleven major battles in World War II from the North African campaign to the landing at Normandy and had been awarded a Bronze Star, President Clinton shook Charlie's hand warmly and came down to Charlie's eye level by sitting on the corner of his desk.

"D-Day, Omaha Beach?" the president asked.

"Utah Beach." Charlie answered. "D-Day plus four."

For the next fifteen minutes Charlie and the president chatted about that fateful day, and I was amazed at one exchange they had. When Charlie first mentioned that his outfit landed on Utah Beach, the president surprised Charlie by asking, "Your outfit took Ste. Marie l'Eglise and St. Malo?"

"Yes," Charlie answered, "how did you know that?"

"I read a lot," said the president, smiling.

By being assigned to Utah Beach instead of being in the first wave of young GIs who stormed Omaha Beach, the men of the First Army's Infantry Divisions missed being among the 52,000 casualties who fell that day.

Charlie talked about how lucky he was to be with the Thirty-seventh Infantry, Ninth Division of the First Army, and wondered why they had been chosen to land on Utah Beach. Charlie's guess was that either the Supreme Allied Command had decided that the soldiers of the First Army needed a break, because they had been in ten major campaigns and were battle weary—or maybe they just tossed a coin.

During the first ten minutes of the President Clinton–Corporal Reiner World War II conversation, a White House aide reminded the president that his helicopter was on the front lawn ready to fly him to New York. The president smiled, said he would be out in a few minutes, and turned his attention back to my brother.

"Charlie," he asked, "did you get to Normandy for the fiftieth anniversary of D-Day?"

Charlie said that he did not.

Wow, I thought, *Charlie and I, in the Oval Office chatting with the president of the United States!* It's at such times that the litany "If only my parents were alive to see this!" pops into my head.

A lot of things have been said and written about President

Clinton, some true, some false, some flattering, some derogatory, some deserved, some not—but that afternoon, I was privy to a moment that allowed me to discover something about President Clinton that I am pleased to pass on.

He described that 50th Anniversary of D-day as being an extraordinarily moving and emotional one for him. He talked about an old friend from his hometown who had accompanied him to the site on which he had stood fifty years earlier. I don't remember the man's name, but this gentleman was one of the many courageous soldiers who clawed their way up the Normandy slopes to engage the enemy. The president related how his friend stood next to him and scanned the thousands of white headstones marking the plots where thousands of our boys were laid to rest.

"After a long moment," the president said, "he pointed to a bluff nearby, and said quietly, 'That's the spot where I saw a bomb hit my brother and blow him to pieces.' He then looked about," the president continued, "and with tears welling up in his eyes, the old man pointed to another area on the hill, and said, 'And over there, a few moments later, I saw my other brother get blown away.' The old gent started to cry like a baby, and it got to me. I couldn't hold back. I just let go and cried with him."

While he was relating this, the president's voice cracked and his eyes filled with tears. He wiped his eyes quickly when his aide came by to remind him that the helicopter was waiting. President Clinton had a few more words for Charlie that I did not hear. He shook his hand, said a blanket good-bye to our family and friends, and left. His eyes were still damp when he shook my hand, and I thought about all the jokes and comments his detractors had made about his use of the phrase, "I feel your pain." He might have overused that phrase, but that day, I saw firsthand and up close a man who had the compassion and the capacity to actually feel someone else's pain.

That day, on October 25 of the year 2000, all of us returned from whence we came, some to New York, some to Los Angeles, and Charlie, Ilse, and their daughter to their home in Atlanta, Georgia.

For the next four months, Charlie and I spoke by phone every day and we discussed his physical condition, the state of the world, and the screwed-up presidential election. Often, we would reminisce about our parents, who had left us many years ago. We thought of how much they would have enjoyed getting the dozens of wonderful photos of President Clinton posing with members of our family. We pictured our mother, Bessie, stuffing those photos in her purse, sitting down on "her bench" in Bronx's Crotona Park and showing off those pictures to all of her friends, acquaintances, and unsuspecting passersby. Charlie and I agreed that it was a miracle of miracles that he was able to make that trip and be at the show. He worried that he might not be around to see it aired. It was to be televised four months hence on the 28th of February.

With the help of his wife and his daughter, caring nurses, and modern medicines, it looked as though he would get to see himself at the Kennedy Center. A couple of days before the show aired, I called to tell him that I had sent a tape of the show by Federal Express so he could play it at his leisure, and he was happy about that. He was also very happy to report that he was feeling wonderful.

"Guess what I did today?" he said, sounding the way he did when he called me from the tuxedo rental store, "I got out of bed, slipped into my shoes, and went outside for a walk."

He had, a couple of months earlier, managed to take a short walk and retrieve the mail from their curbside mailbox.

"Charlie, you're kidding! You actually felt well enough to walk down to the mailbox?"

"Not to the mailbox," he said proudly, "to the street. I walked on the road, and without my cane. I went for about half a mile."

"That's a long walk."

"You're telling me? I was too tired to walk back!"

"How did you get back?"

"Elaine picked me up with the car . . . I was pooped!"

Incredible as it seemed, I believed him, I guess because I wanted to believe that he was getting better.

A few minutes later when I spoke with Ilse and my niece, Elaine, they told me that the half-mile walk was in his mind.

"But," I argued, "he sounds exactly like himself!"

They explained that he went in and out of fantasy, and that he got very tired and went to sleep very early every night. They were glad that the tape of the show was coming the following morning, because mornings were when he was most alert. They didn't think he would be able to stay awake until nine o'clock to see it on television.

Charlie did not get to see himself on tape or on television. He didn't get to see himself looking handsome in his rented tuxedo or hear again all the lovely things I was moved to say about him. He passed away early that morning.

Corporal Charles Reiner was given a military funeral with full honors at Arlington National Cemetery on March 4, 2001. He was eighty-two years and three months old, and he is missed.